ETHICS and VALUES

VOLUME 6
Marriage–Punishment

Grolier Educational

Published 1999 by Grolier Educational
Sherman Turnpike
Danbury, Connecticut 06816

Set ISBN: 0-7172-9274-6
Volume ISBN: 0-7172-9280-0

Library of Congress Cataloging-in-Publication Data
Ethics and values.
        p. cm.
    Includes bibliographical references and index.
    Contents: v. 1. Abortion–censorship—v. 2. Character–crime—v. 3. Criticism–fairness—v. 4. Family–honor—v. 5. Hope–lying—v. 6. Marriage–punishment—v. 7. Racism–slander—v. 8. Smoking–wrong.
    Summary: Presents brief articles on a wide range of issues related to ethics, morals, and values.
    1. Ethics—Encyclopedias, Juvenile. 2. Values—Encyclopedias, Juvenile. [1. Ethics—Encyclopedias. 2. Values—Encyclopedias.]
I. Grolier Education Corporation.
BJ63.E544 1998   98-18069
170.3—dc21   CIP
                                                      AC

For Brown Partworks Ltd
Consultant: Ronald F. Reed, President, International Council for
    Philosophical Inquiry with Children, Texas Wesleyan University
Project editor: Dawn Titmus
Designer: Sandra Horth
Text editor: Robert Anderson
Picture research: Brigitte Arora

Printed in Singapore

Contributors: Ashley Brown, Lesley Coia, Crerar Douglas, Margaret Doyle, Adriana Fresquet, James Goss, Leon Gray, Maughn Gregory, Philip Guin, Casey Horton, Doris Jones, James Kellenberger, David Kennedy, Walter Kohan, Thomas Mahoney, Michael Pritchard, David Robins, Henry Russell, Ann Margaret Sharp, Laurance Splitter, Mark Weinstein, Ian Westwell, Robert Youngson.

Contents

Introduction

Ethics and Values is intended to help students come to grips with important issues of morality that bear on all of our lives. When questions arise about the rights and wrongs of abortion, capital punishment, euthanasia, and many other difficult or troubling aspects of life and death, it is important to be able to turn to an unbiased source of information and advice. As we all know, figuring out in a particular instance what is the right way to behave is not always easy. To see the issues for what they really are is certainly the best way to begin to work out a course of action—and a code of behavior.

As well as providing clear, concise information about issues of practical morality, *Ethics and Values* also looks behind personal value systems at the religious, philosophical, and political teachings that underpin so many of our beliefs. How does the Christian message differ from the teachings of Islam? How do capitalist and communist systems affect the way people behave toward one another?

Ethics and Values provides a rounded survey of the field of ethical belief and behavior. The entries are arranged A-Z with extensive cross-referencing, making it an easy-to-use ready reference.

Marriage

Traditionally, when a man and a woman promise in a religious or civil ceremony to love and care for each other now and in the future, their relationship is a marriage.

What Is Marriage For?

In the past the purpose of marriage was to bestow God's blessing on a couple's sexual relationship. Marriage was also a way of giving the relationship social recognition. With this recognition came certain rights and responsibilities for the couple.

Although our view of what marriage means has changed in the 20th century, most people still consider it to be a contract between a woman and a man who promise to love and care for one another.

Today, though, the term "marriage" covers a broader range of relationships. In Western societies some people use the term to refer to the relationships of couples who live together but have never married, as well as to the relationships of same-sex couples.

Although same-sex "marriages" are generally not legally recognized in the United States (Hawaii is the only exception at present), they are often recognized socially. The family and friends of the "married" couple treat the two as if they are married. Usually the two people concerned have been living together for a long time and have publicly declared their commitment to one another.

Types of Marriage

Although every human society has some form of marriage, marriage varies enormously across cultures. For example, in the past many societies have approved of a man having more than one wife at the same time. In a few cultures women are allowed to have more than one husband.

People also differ in how they choose their marriage partner. In some societies parents choose spouses on behalf of their children. These arranged marriages, as they are called, can be a way to maintain links between families and for parents to insure their children's prosperity and well-being.

In all societies, though, there are restrictions on who can marry whom. In the United States, for instance, it is illegal for a person to marry his or her first cousin or brother or sister (sibling).

Income, social class, profession, religion, race, and education all play a part in what people look for in a marriage partner. Sometimes people get married to someone who is richer or of a higher class than they are. In these cases marriage may be a stepping stone to greater wealth or higher status.

More often, though, people tend to marry others who have a background or status similar to their own, although studies have shown that this does not necessarily guarantee a successful marriage.

Why Marry?

People's reasons for marrying vary, including wanting to make a public commitment to each other and the desire to raise a family together. The romantic ideal of marrying for love is certainly one reason, but some people do not consider this to be the wisest basis for a lifelong commitment. In arranged marriages the families hope that love will develop between the partners over time.

Traditionally, marriage was important to establish a stable unit in which to raise children. Today, though, marriage does not always result in children; the number of couples choosing to remain childless is on the increase. And many children are born outside marriage, either because the parents never married or because the mother lives alone.

These people are celebrating their 50th wedding anniversary. In traditional Christian marriage vows people promise to stay together "till death do us part."

Most people who marry intend to stay with that partner for the rest of their lives. But the reality is that in the United States more than half of first-time marriages end in divorce. In spite of the divorce statistics, though, most adults choose to marry at some time in their lives; and although divorce rates are high, so are rates of remarriage.

The Value of Marriage

Many people are disturbed about the extent to which marriage in modern society has changed. They believe, for instance, that it is too easy for people to get divorced and that we no longer value marriage. They say that marriage has lost its meaning. Others say that marriage breakdown and single-parent families contribute to social problems such as crime and delinquency.

Is marriage important? Do we need it as evidence of a couple's commitment? Some people argue that marriage is still important because it is a public declaration of commitment that people are more likely to keep than if they simply live together.

Others argue that the things we as a society value about marriage—such as loyalty, protection, love, friendship, companionship, and sharing—can apply equally to people who are not married. The ability to enjoy a deep and lasting community does not depend on the legal status of a couple's relationship, they say.

SEE ALSO: DIVORCE, FAMILY, MONOGAMY, PARENTING, PROMISES, RELATIONSHIPS, SEXUAL BEHAVIOR, VALUES.

Media

The media made sure that Diana, princess of Wales, was constantly in the public eye. Some people argue that her constant exposure to the media contributed to the collapse of her marriage and even to her death in a high-speed car chase in 1997.

The channels by which information (including news, ideas, and opinions) is supplied to a society are collectively known as the media. Television, radio, newspapers, magazines, advertising, photographs, and movies are all examples of media.

A Channel for Criticism and Debate

Freedom of information and opinion is essential to any democratic society. We have to be able to criticize the decisions made by those who govern us and to be able to debate freely the important issues that affect our lives and happiness.

One of the roles of the media is to act as a channel for this criticism and debate. In order to perform this role, the media have to be as accessible (open) as possible. That is, as many people as possible should be able to use the media, both to air their own views and to find out about those of others. The media also need to be impartial. In other words, they should reflect the fullest range of opinions without prejudice.

Because the media play such a vital role in democracy, in one-party countries such as China governments usually own and strictly control newspapers and television.

In the United States the legal system aims to insure the freedom of the media through the First Amendment. "Congress," says the First Amendment, "shall make no law…abridging [restricting] the freedom of speech, or of the press."

However, the freedom of the press has to be balanced against other constitutional rights and freedoms. For example, the law recognizes that libel (lies written down with the intent to harm) and national security are valid reasons for censoring or criticizing the media. Other less legitimate pressures also work to limit media freedom, however.

Undermining Democracy

Like any industry the media are guided by profit. Media corporations sell for millions of dollars. Well-established organizations are swallowing up smaller companies that cannot afford to compete.

In Western countries the media are becoming concentrated in the hands of a few rich and powerful owners. The international media mogul Rupert Murdoch, for example, owns local and national newspapers, magazines, TV networks, film studios, and book publishers in many countries.

Critics suggest that such powerful owners secretly lay down rules about what does and does not get reported in the media. They may do this, critics say, to maximize their profits or to influence political decisions or even the course of justice.

A newspaper owner, for example, may encourage journalists to withhold information from the public when a story seems to threaten the interests of his company. Similarly, he may give front-page coverage to a political scandal that seems likely to damage a political party he is opposed to.

As well, the concentration of the media in the hands of so few people may mean that the media are reflecting an increasingly narrow range of views. Critics argue that we think we are getting a diversity of opinion when, in fact, we are not. The media, they say, are undermining democracy.

Press Intrusion

Some people argue that the media have too much freedom. Such arguments usually focus on the intrusion of the press into the private lives of "personalities" such as film stars or politicians. The media's treatment of Diana, princess of Wales, which included constant harassment by journalists and photographers, is a recent example of what some consider to be the abuse of press freedom.

Many people think that legislation (laws) should safeguard public figures from press intrusion. Others view media attention as an inevitable part of a celebrity's life. Some argue, too, that the public has a right to know when, for example, a politician's private life jars with his or her public policy.

SEE ALSO: CENSORSHIP, DEMOCRACY, LIBEL, POLITICAL CONDUCT, PORNOGRAPHY, POWER, PRIVACY, SPYING.

ETHICS ON THE NET

The Internet seems to fulfill the ideal of freedom of information for all safeguarded in the First Amendment. Many thinkers argue that because it promotes free debate among people from all over the globe, it is a strong tool for democracy.

But the Internet also raises serious ethical issues. Many people believe, for example, that users, and children in particular, should be protected from the racist and pornographic material available on the Net. Others wonder, too, whether it is ethical to lie on the Net. Is it right, for example, for a man to say he is a woman?

However, many people argue that by censoring the Net, we will get rid of its democratic potential. As with other media a balance has to be found between the claims of free speech and other human rights.

Medical Ethics

The branch of philosophy concerned with the way doctors behave and make moral decisions when they are dealing with their patients is called medical ethics.

Medical Codes

The term "medical ethics" was first used in 1803, when British physician Thomas Percival published a book called *Medical Ethics*. In this book Percival described his ideas about how he thought physicians and surgeons ought to behave.

The idea of medical ethics, however, goes back long before the start of the 19th century. The Greek physician Hippocrates, who was born about 460 B.C. and who is called the "Father of Medicine," gave his name to an oath that doctors have followed ever since. Many medical students are still required to take this oath when they graduate.

The Hippocratic Oath has two main sections. The first deals with the relationship of the doctor with her students, while in the second section the doctor promises, among other things, to prescribe only beneficial drugs and to refrain from any harmful action.

In 1948 the World Medical Association (WMA) drew up a version of the Hippocratic Oath called "The Geneva Declaration." This covers much the same points as the original oath. Most doctors take these principles very seriously and will, for instance, refuse to reveal secrets obtained during medical consultations, even in a court of law.

The influence of the ancient Greek physician Hippocrates on both the science and ethics of medicine continues to be felt today.

Doctors' Dilemmas

The whole basis of medical practice, according to the Hippocratic Oath, is to save life. However, changing social values and rapid advances in medicine have made it increasingly harder for doctors to live by such a straightforward code of ethics.

Doctors consequently often find themselves bearing the brunt of some of the most heated ethical debates of our day. For example, in the original Hippocratic Oath the doctor swore "not to give to a woman a pill

to produce abortion." Today many people, including the majority of doctors, believe that women should have the right to choose whether or not to have an abortion, and accordingly many countries have legalized abortion. Some people, however, argue that the doctor who carries out an abortion is breaking his professional creed—that is, his duty to preserve life.

"Deadly Medicine"

Many would say that the issue of euthanasia ("mercy killing") presents the doctor with an even more acute moral dilemma. A person dying from a very painful disease may, for example, beg his doctor to bring about his death artificially. Such an act not only goes against the Hippocratic ban on giving "deadly medicine," but in most countries it is against the law.

The doctor has to decide whether she is prepared to sacrifice her professional creed (and perhaps even her career) out of compassion for her patient. Evidence suggests that many doctors are prepared to make this sacrifice. And many people who support euthanasia argue that it is unfair that society passes the responsibility for making such decisions on to doctors.

Some people point out that society is sometimes guilty of double standards when faced with the idea of a doctor administering lethal doses of drugs. Whereas all American states forbid euthanasia, many of them require a doctor to be present when criminals are executed. The WMA has condemned doctors' presence at executions as unethical.

The Ethics of Medical Research

During World War II doctors working for the German Nazi regime (1933–1945) carried out medical experiments on the inmates of concentration camps. The most infamous of these Nazi physicians was Josef Mengele (1911–1979), who as the chief doctor of the Birkenau camp was nicknamed "the Angel of Death." Mengele supervised cruel experiments on Jews in order to find ways of increasing the fertility of the German race.

Mengele's terrible crimes alerted the civilized world to the responsibilities attached to medical research. In 1964 the WMA set out a code of principles that was intended to guide doctors who were involved in such research projects as the clinical testing of new drugs on patients.

One of these principles was that the patient should be likely to benefit directly from the research and not be expected to take risks for an unknown gain in medical knowledge. Some people argue that this principle ought to be extended to include experimentation on animals.

SEE ALSO: ABORTION, ANIMAL RIGHTS, DEATH, DUTY, EUTHANASIA, HOLOCAUST, KILLING, NAZISM, PARENTING.

THE GENEVA DECLARATION

Many doctors are expected to swear a modern version of the Hippocratic Oath called the Geneva Declaration, part of which reads:

…I solemnly pledge myself to consecrate my life to the service of humanity; I will give my teachers the respect and gratitude which is their due; I will practice my profession with conscience and with dignity. The health of my patient will be my first consideration; I will respect the secrets which are confided in me; I will maintain by all the means in my power, the honor and the noble traditions of the medical profession…

Minorities

A small group of people that differs in some way from everybody else (the majority) in a society is called a minority. Race, religion, politics, disability, and sexuality are just a few of the important ways in which minorities differ from the majority in a society or community.

Types of Minority

There are many examples of religious minorities. Small religious communities such as the Amish have fought hard to keep their way of life in a sometimes hostile society. Pride in their history and origins helps religious minorities survive.

Sometimes the difference is sexual. A minority of men and women in society are homosexual (gay). Once they were virtual outcasts, but now societies generally recognize the rights of gay people. Every year Gay Pride marches are held in San Francisco, New York, London, Sydney, Paris, and in many other cities of the world.

A Melting Pot

The United States has long been a haven for minorities. Today out of a total population of 261 million, there are some 30 million African Americans, 22 million Hispanics, 7 million Asians, and 1.5 million Native Americans in the United States. Three hundred years ago Native Americans were the majority.

Many of these minorities were escaping persecution. The British writer Israel Zangwill (1864–1926) called America "a melting pot." He thought that in time all these different peoples would forget their own identities and integrate into the American way of life.

However, many members of minority ethnic communities complain that even when they do attempt to integrate, they often meet with prejudice and rejection. Many feel that even when they try to be "American," people still see them first of all as "black" or "Hispanic." There is also evidence that nonwhite ethnic minorities are discriminated against in the job market.

In the 1960s civil-rights leaders such as Martin Luther King Jr. (1929–1968) encouraged African Americans to take pride in their identity. Since then many people belonging to ethnic minorities have argued that minority groups should have the right to keep their own values and way of life—that is, to remain outside mainstream American society.

The Trouble with Minorities

To many the word "minority" spells trouble. It means people with placards protesting long-standing grievances. Such people have been dubbed the "vocal minority." Minorities are often unpopular with what former American President Richard Nixon called the "silent majority." Minority views can sometimes be seen as questioning or even threatening the values of the rest of society.

In the world today minority issues are a major cause of war. For example, on the island of Sri Lanka, off the southern tip of India, there has been fighting since 1983 between the majority, who are Buddhist, and the minority Tamils, who are Hindu.

Minorities everywhere are often in great physical danger. In the 1990s in the Central African country of Rwanda extremists from the majority Hutu people tried to wipe out

Each of us is probably a member of some kind of minority because of our religion, race, or even our taste in clothes. Whether we belong to a majority or a minority, we all have to live together.

the Tutsi minority. The Marsh Arabs have lived in southern Iraq for more than 5,000 years. Today their ancient lifestyle is threatened by the genocidal (race-murdering) policies of Iraqi leader Saddam Hussein.

Sometimes, however, the position is reversed: a minority of people can control unfairly the lives of the majority. In South Africa for many decades three million whites tried to dominate 30 million blacks.

The Right to Be Different
Today such cities as New York, Chicago, and Los Angeles are increasingly multicultural. In the schools and colleges of New York, for example, students speak some 40 different languages. However, economic and social tensions can sometimes erupt in violence. This happened, for instance, in the Los Angeles riots of 1992. Often, though, the peaceful interaction between minorities and majority can enrich all our lives.

People take great pride in being members of a minority. The right to be different is very important. To protect the rights of minorities, whatever their differences, is one of the most important tasks of a democratic society.

SEE ALSO: AFFIRMATIVE ACTION, COMMUNITY, DISCRIMINATION, IDENTITY, OPPRESSION, PREJUDICE, PRIDE, RACISM, RIGHTS, SEXISM, TOLERANCE.

Modesty

When sea bathing became popular in Britain in the 19th century, "bathing machines" (cabins on wheels) enabled women to bathe in private, away from prying male eyes.

A modest person is one who is neither conceited nor vain but who behaves in a quiet or unassuming way. The term "modest" can also describe someone who dresses "appropriately"; that is, in a socially acceptable way. Both senses of the term describe a person who does not "show off."

A Religious Virtue

Traditionally, modesty has been a religious virtue, particularly for women. In the 1st century A.D. St. Paul wrote to Timothy that "women should adorn [decorate] themselves modestly and sensibly in seemly apparel [appropriate clothing]." The Christian thinker St. Augustine of Hippo (A.D. 354–430) went further and even condemned makeup for women, except in private to please their husbands.

Throughout history governments have used "sumptuary laws" to control extravagant spending. Most of these laws restricted the type of fabrics and outfits people could wear. Often the laws aimed to maintain class or status differences between people, but sometimes there were moral reasons, too.

King Edward III of England (1312–1377), for instance, ruled that no person below the rank of knight was allowed to wear fur. And both Edward IV of England (1442–1483) and Henry III of France (1551–1589) issued sumptuary laws because, they said, God was displeased with people's extravagant clothing.

In many Islamic societies today women are expected to show modesty in their dress. The Islamic sacred book, the Koran, gives guidance on this, but it is not a strict ruling. The all-male governments in some Islamic countries, however, insist that women cover themselves from head to toe and veil their faces when they go out in public.

Many feminists argue that in Islamic and Western societies, valuing female modesty has become a way of oppressing women. Modesty is a way of keeping women "in their place"—that is, subordinate to men and without real power—they say.

Modest Behavior

Today in Western societies we tend to focus on behavior more than dress when we think about modesty. We say that a modest person is one who has learned to put her ego in perspective. In other words, she sees herself —her skills and failings, vices and virtues— as she truly is. She has no need to "blow her own trumpet" to make herself feel valued or to think of herself as a good person.

A person who has learned to put her ego in perspective is not weak. She does not pretend to be humble (lacking in vanity or boastfulness). On the contrary, she has a well-balanced sense of self—she is neither too humble nor too boastful.

A modest person is someone who is capable of making a good judgment about what behavior is fitting or appropriate. She has the ability to think beyond herself about the consequences of her actions and behavior on others.

At the same time, modest individuals tend to celebrate the ordinary rather than the extraordinary in life. In other words, they see the extraordinary in the ordinary.

Competition and Modesty

Yet in many ways our capitalist societies do not encourage us to be modest. Instead, we are taught that we must be competitive and learn to "sell ourselves"—to flaunt our skills—if we are to get on and succeed in the world. Often we think of modest people as those who do not push themselves forward, who are shy, and therefore not successful.

On the other hand, many of us appreciate and admire modesty in others. From an early age we learn that boastful people are not fun to be with. Someone who is constantly boasting about his achievements or telling us how skillful he is quickly becomes someone we do not want to spend time with. In other words, vain or conceited people do not seem to care much for us and our talents—they want only our admiration.

Learning to Be Modest

Learning to be modest is not an easy task. One way that children can learn the skills of modest behavior is by participating in a classroom community of inquiry. In such an environment they realize that they have to take turns, listen to others, build on the ideas of others, and consider their ideas in relationship to others' ideas. They learn the importance of inquiring in a cooperative way about issues.

SEE ALSO: BEAUTY, CONCEIT, HUMILITY, INQUIRY, SELF-ESTEEM, VANITY, VIRTUE.

Monogamy

Many people in Western societies value monogamy and believe that a marriage should be a lifelong commitment to one's spouse or partner.

The term "monogamy" literally means "one marriage," and traditionally monogamy meant marrying only once in a lifetime. Nowadays, though, the term refers to marriages or relationships in which each person has only one spouse (husband or wife) or sexual partner at any one time.

Monogamy and Polygamy

Monogamy has been the ideal in Western culture since pre-Christian times. Traditionally, however, many societies have preferred polygamy, a practice that allows those people who can afford it to have more than one spouse at the same time. Usually, these societies favored polygyny, in which one man has more than one wife. A few societies practiced polyandry, in which women could have more than one husband.

Polygamy is still practiced in many cultures today. Yet even in cultures that have traditionally practiced some form of polygamy, monogamy is becoming the norm. One reason for this is that the Christian missionaries who traveled throughout the world spreading the Christian doctrine taught that monogamy is the only married state recognized by God. The increasing influence of Western culture has also led more people to practice monogamy.

Serial Monogamy and Bigamy

Many adults in Western societies have more than one spouse during their lifetime, either because of the death of a spouse or because of divorce. The practice of having one spouse after another is called "serial monogamy" since it involves people having a series of spouses, but one at a time.

Bigamy is the act of getting married to one person while still legally being married to another. It is illegal in the United States and other countries in which polygamy is also against the law.

Bigamy usually means that the person who marries twice deceives both of his or her spouses. The second spouse usually enters the marriage in good faith, believing it to be a lawful marriage.

Monogamy and Religious Beliefs

When monogamy is an ideal in a society, one question is under what conditions a marriage can end. The Catholic Church forbids divorce, for instance, except in very special circumstances. And many Hindus believe that a marriage does not end even when one of the spouses dies.

Hindus have often believed marriage to extend beyond death. Traditionally, when a man died, his widow would be cremated alive, usually willingly, on his funeral pyre so that the two could be together in death. This practice was known as "suttee." It was made illegal in British India in 1829, although it continued for some years after.

Monogamous Values Today

Traditionally, people have viewed marriage as a stable social unit within which parents can raise their children. Many people argue that when marriages break up, the children suffer the most. Some studies have shown, for instance, that children from "broken" homes are more likely to be delinquent.

For these reasons, among others, Western cultures continue to value monogamy today. Most people would agree that being monogamous builds trust in a relationship. They argue that because marriage is, or should be, a lifelong commitment, adultery (having sexual partners outside marriage) puts this commitment at risk.

Some religious thinkers have argued that monogamy is humans' natural state. It is difficult, if not impossible, to determine whether this is so, but many people argue that it is unrealistic to expect people to remain monogamous. Sexual relationships outside of marriage are commonplace and even accepted among some members of society.

Some people, for instance, believe that "open marriages"—in which both spouses agree it is acceptable for them to have other sexual partners—are healthier because they permit the open and honest expression of people's sexual needs. Open marriages became popular among certain sections of U.S. society in the 1960s and 1970s. This was a time when people were challenging tradition and exploring new ways of living.

Most people today, however, would probably argue that monogamy still has value. They might point out that loyalty and trust are important in any relationship, and particularly in marriage.

SEE ALSO: DIVORCE, FAMILY, LIFESTYLES, MARRIAGE, PARENTING, SEXUAL BEHAVIOR.

Morality

Accepted ideas about right and wrong in a society are collectively called its moral code, or morality. Usually societies reward individuals when they conform to a moral code and punish them when they transgress (go against) it.

Morality and Society

Every society has a strong system of beliefs about how its members should behave. When people share a moral code, it is easier for them to live together. For example, in nearly all societies it is considered wrong (immoral) to kill other people except in self-defense. A belief such as this is usually made into a law, so that an individual who offends against his society's morality by killing someone can be legally punished.

Some aspects of a society's morality, however, are not made into laws. For example, many societies believe that it is wrong for married people to commit adultery—to have sexual partners other than their spouse. If individuals break this moral code, they may suffer criticism from others but are not usually punished by the law.

Different societies have different ideas about which transgressions merit criticism and which merit punishment. For example, although Western societies do not usually punish adulterers, some Islamic countries do so by stoning them to death.

Learning Moral Codes

In every society adults teach children a set of moral rules (a moral code). For example, parents teach their children that it is wrong to tell lies and that it is right to be kind to other people. In this way children learn which behaviors are valued in their society.

Children do not learn a moral code only by following rules, however. They also learn from watching the behavior of adults—their parents and teachers, for example. If adults act in accordance with their moral code—by being unselfish, honest, and kind, for example—it is much more likely that children will adopt this behavior, too.

On the other hand, if the adults around them behave selfishly, tell lies, or are unkind, children will often notice that there is a difference between what adults teach in theory and what they actually do in practice.

This gap between theory and practice can be harmful. A child who sees that a moral code is only for show may be tempted to ignore most of it.

Morality and Hypocrisy

Sometimes morality can be more a matter of convention (what is generally agreed on) than of deeply held beliefs. As a consequence, when our moral code is put to the test, we sometimes find that we have only been paying lip service to our society's morality.

That is, we may discover that we have no real conviction that a moral belief is actually right and that we have held that belief only because it is what society expects.

For example, a man may believe that all people are equal and yet be angry when his son or daughter decides to marry a person from a different class or race. We usually say that this man is guilty of hypocrisy—that is, of saying one thing while doing another.

We are usually particularly sensitive to hypocrisy in public figures such as politicians. For example, we would probably have a low opinion of a congresswoman who, while supporting family values in public, was found to be acting in a way that went against those values in private.

Being a moral person means more than simply following the given moral rules of a society. We have to think carefully about

moral issues and decide for ourselves whether we really do consider something to be wrong or whether, in fact, we are merely following a widely held prejudice.

For example, for a long time people considered homosexuality to be morally wrong, and it could be punished under the law. Since the 1960s, however, people have questioned moral codes that interfere with individuals' private lives (their lifestyles). Today most people respect individuals' right to be homosexual.

Morality and Religion

Many people look to religion to provide them with a moral code. The great religions of the world can provide profound insights into our moral responsibility as human beings, both to each other and to God.

In the 18th century the English philosopher John Locke (1632–1704) argued that morality always depends on religion. He believed that a person who had no religion could have no morality. Atheists, he argued, are moral outlaws.

Even today some people argue that the lack of religious faith in modern society has brought about a collapse in moral values and led to social problems such as drug abuse and unwanted pregnancies.

However, some thinkers have pointed out that human beings can have a strong moral code without necessarily believing in God. Humanism, for example, is a philosophy that usually rejects the notion of a supreme being and yet believes that we should live by firm moral principles.

SEE ALSO: CONDUCT, CRIME, DUTY, ETHICS, EVIL, GOOD, HONOR, HUMANISM, IDEALS, LAW, PUNISHMENT, RELIGION, RESPONSIBILITY, RULES, SIN, TRADITION, VALUES, VIRTUE, WRONG.

Nationalism

The term "nationalism" generally refers to the loyalty and devotion that a group of people feel toward their nation. It can also mean that those people consider their nation to be superior to other nations, and that they promote the interests and culture of their nation over those of other nations.

What Is a Nation?

A nation, or state, usually covers a distinct geographical area that is defined by internationally agreed borders. A nation must be free from any outside political interference in its domestic affairs. At the same time, it has a right because of its nationhood to be treated as an equal partner by other nations in diplomatic negotiations.

Nationalism as an idea evolved in the 18th century. French writer Jean-Jacques Rousseau (1712–1778), for instance, argued that states ruled by a monarch (king or queen) or by small minorities for whom the people had not voted (unrepresentative elites) were undemocratic. He believed that such states survived only by oppressing the majority, the ordinary people.

Rousseau and others argued that the state could survive only if ordinary citizens had some kind of voice in its running. If ordinary people could elect representatives through ballots, have protection under the law, and understand their obligations, then a stronger state would emerge, he said.

The French Revolution

Nationalism found one of its first expressions during the French Revolution (1789–1799). Inspired by the ideas of such writers as

The Basque people are extremely proud of their culture, and many of them would like to see an independent Basque nation. This boy is wearing the traditional Basque costume.

Rousseau, the French people overthrew the old, undemocratic order by executing the king and his nobles, established a democracy, and then willingly went to war against other undemocratic European countries to protect their new freedoms.

In the modern world nationalist movements have acted as a focal point for those living under colonial rule who feel such rule to be exploitative (harms their interests).

The North Vietnamese, for example, fought first against the French and then against the United States to rid their divided country of foreign interference. Their aim was to create a united country, which they succeeded in doing in 1975.

A Binding Force

Nationalism has been a way of binding people together by general consent. People have rights (freedom from persecution, for example) but also obligations. These might include the obligation to pay taxes, to obey the law, or to go to war to protect the home country if it is threatened.

At the most basic level people express their support for the nation by such acts as saluting the national flag, singing the national anthem, and cheering for a national team in an international sporting event.

However, few countries are "pure" examples of the nation-state. Many countries contain minorities that have distinctively different cultures or are members of a different ethnic group from the majority. These minorities might speak different languages and have different religions.

Some nations are sufficiently open and democratic to guarantee their minorities equal rights. Others are not so democratic or appear not to be to those who consider themselves an oppressed minority.

Nationalistic Violence

Nationalists in some minority groups use democratic means to achieve their aims. But others have turned to violence.

In Canada, for instance, many French speakers in the province of Quebec, where they are a majority, support a political party that campaigns for greater independence from the national government. In the 1970s, however, a few French speakers turned to violence to achieve total independence. And in Spain the Basque terrorist group ETA uses violence, including bombings, to win an independent homeland for the Basque people.

History has shown that nationalism can be a positive political force, creating a united, democratic nation. But nationalism can also be a force for conflict and violence.

SEE ALSO: CITIZENSHIP, DEMOCRACY, EXTREMISM, FASCISM, MINORITIES, NAZISM, OPPRESSION, PATRIOTISM, VIOLENCE.

EXTREME NATIONALISM

Extreme nationalism has often been used by some leaders to control their peoples and wage aggressive wars that have nothing to do with protecting the nation. By focusing on real or imagined threats to the nation, they have suspended or swept away the people's rights. The threats may be from a foreign power or from an "enemy within."

Many modern right-wing military dictatorships, particularly in Latin America, have suspended democratic rights and used violence to silence opposition, supposedly for the national good. They have also used nationalist causes to hide corruption and maladministration in their own regimes by focusing their people's frustrations on external threats.

Nazism

The ideology and policies of the Nazi Party, which was in power in Germany from 1933 to 1945 under the leadership of Adolf Hitler (1889–1945), are known as Nazism. By the end of World War II (1939–1945) the Nazis had inflicted horror on a massive scale on the peoples of Europe.

A Popular Political Party

Between the early 1920s and 1933 Hitler transformed the Nazis from a right-wing fringe movement into a major political party. His political philosophy drew heavily on political ideas that had been widespread throughout Europe for much of the 19th century—chiefly aggressive nationalism, anti-Semitism, and racism. He was also inspired by the fascist regime of Italian dictator Benito Mussolini (1883–1945).

After Germany was defeated in World War I, the German economy was in ruins with runaway inflation and high unemployment, and there was great political turmoil. Hitler offered the German people solutions and explanations in uncertain times.

Hitler believed that Germany's defeat in World War I was due not to military failure but to the so-called "stab in the back." Corrupt politicians, communists, extremists, and Jews, among others, were responsible for Germany's defeat and its postwar economic and political problems, he said.

A huge crowd of Nazi soldiers listens to a speech by Hitler during a rally at Nuremberg, in Germany, in 1936. Hitler used these rallies to instill in his troops loyalty and obedience.

Hitler promised to make Germany strong again both economically and militarily, to destroy those he blamed for the postwar problems, and to create a regime that could not be challenged by any external power. He intended to build an empire in Europe that would last for 1,000 years.

A One-Party State

Hitler's message was highly popular, and in March 1933 the Nazis won 44 percent of the vote. However, the Nazis used democratic processes only for their own ends; essentially, they were antidemocratic. They used violence to silence political opponents, and in 1933 Hitler seized power.

Once in power the Nazis set about turning Germany into a one-party state. They banned all rival political parties, and there were no more elections.

If the one-party Nazi state was to survive, Hitler believed Germany had to be completely remolded. To get the German people to adopt Nazi values, the Nazis used propaganda (strategies to persuade others of a viewpoint), state-controlled media, and a Nazi-dominated education program. They wanted to "purify" the German culture and rejected anything that was not German.

Traditional Roles

Hitler believed that German men and women should take on traditional roles. Men were workers, soldiers, and holders of power. The position of women was summed up in the phrase "*Kinder, Kirche, Kuche,*" which means "children, church, kitchen." The Nazis rewarded women for having large families but made it more difficult for them to go to college. They were deliberately excluded from working in politics, the army, the labor market, and the justice system.

Those who did not fit neatly into these roles, including homosexuals, were persecuted or "eliminated" (killed).

Germans who objected to the regime faced being arrested and tried. The flip side to the Nazi promises of economic, political, and social stability was the loss of personal freedom, mainly the right to free expression, choice, and access to democratic processes.

Hitler also attempted to "purify" Europe. He believed that the mixing of races had weakened Germany and that first Germany and then Europe had to be "made fit" for the Aryan race (to which the Germans belonged). He believed Aryans had a right to European lands and that if Nazi Germany was to grow strong, it needed to take over and settle lands occupied by non-Aryans. This was the idea behind Germany's invasion of Poland in 1939, which led, ultimately, to war.

As part of their "purification" policy the Nazis sent people to extermination (death) camps. In the camps Nazis murdered some six million European Jews and countless homosexuals, Romanies (Gypsies), and other people they saw as racially inferior.

Neo-Nazism Today

The Nazi ideology continues to attract some people today. These neo-Nazis, as they are called, see Hitler's beliefs as an answer to their own problems. Many are poorly educated and are economically disadvantaged. With only a few exceptions they rely on threats, intimidation, and violence to make a point. Their anger is often directed against governments, ethnic minorities, foreign visitors, and those who speak out for tolerance.

SEE ALSO: ANTI-SEMITISM, FASCISM, GENOCIDE, HOLOCAUST, MINORITIES, NATIONALISM, OPPRESSION, TOLERANCE, VIOLENCE, WAR.

Obedience

When we do what someone in authority tells us to do—that is, when we follow their orders—we are showing obedience.

An Old-fashioned Virtue?
People once believed that obedience was a necessary virtue. It was thought of as a kind of glue that held society together. People of a lower class were expected to obey those of a higher class; women were expected to obey men; children were expected to obey their parents; and all humans were expected to obey God. Without obedience, people thought, society would fall apart.

Army recruits undergo basic training at Fort Dix, New Jersey. In the military obedience is vital if soldiers are to work together as an effective fighting force.

At the same time, people considered disobedience to be wrong or even sinful. According to Christian thought, the first human beings sinned out of disobedience. In the Bible Adam and Eve disobey God by eating from the Tree of Knowledge, and God punishes them by driving them out of the Garden of Eden. Disobedience is the origin of human suffering, some Christians think.

Today, however, we have become mistrustful of authority, in part because of historical examples of the abuse of power and in part because of democratic ideas about equality and freedom. Whatever the cause, we no longer believe that we have an automatic duty to defer (give way) to those who claim to be our "betters."

However, some people argue that our society would be better off if we were more even-handed in our attitude toward obedience and learned to judge when it is appropriate for us to obey and when it is not.

Parents and Children

Parents, when they are angry, sometimes say such things as "I expect you to obey me." Certainly we owe them obedience when they know better or when it is an accepted family rule. We obey our parents usually because we trust them to know what is best for us.

Traditionally, many sorts of obedience derive their justification from this model of the relationship between parents and children. God has been called "our father," kings and queens were once seen as the fathers and mothers of their people, and schools traditionally make rules for students *in loco parentis*—that is, in place of parents.

Obedience and the Law

Many people, however, see a clearer model for obedience in the law. One obvious reason why we obey the law is that society threatens to punish us if we do not. We obey laws partly out of fear and partly because it is in our own interests to do so.

When we obey laws—especially good laws—we are helping create a harmonious society. Good laws benefit society and its members because they meet the needs of the members of the society.

This helps us understand why we owe obedience to our "betters." We assume that our parents or teachers have established rules and make demands that are prompted by their greater wisdom and concern for us.

Civil Disobedience

Sometimes, however, we may believe that a law is unjust or that it conflicts with our conscience. In a free society, of course, we can use the democratic process to campaign for a change in the law. But what if we lived under a government that denied us our full rights or in some way sidelined our interests?

When our rights are consistently ignored and we sincerely believe in the correctness of our cause, then some people would argue that we have a right to disobey those laws that oppress or exclude us. We usually call this practice "civil disobedience."

Civil disobedience has been successfully practiced by Indians living under British colonial rule, African Americans living under segregation laws in the United States, and AIDS activists faced with public indifference to the death of thousands of homosexual men. Some of the great heroes of the 20th century practiced civil disobedience, including Mahatma Gandhi (1869–1948) and Martin Luther King Jr. (1929–1968).

Some people have argued, however, that the logical extension of civil disobedience is anarchy and that for this reason it is wrong. How do we know when to resist or when to see the wisdom and virtue of obedience? Clearly, we need to be sure that a law violates some fundamental principle or right such as treating people fairly or freedom of speech.

SEE ALSO: CITIZENSHIP, CRIME, DEMOCRACY, DUTY, FEMINISM, LAW, OPPRESSION, PROTEST, RACISM, RIGHTS, TREASON.

Oppression

When people are not free to do as they wish because others are in control of their lives, they are the victims of oppression.

A Fact of Life?

Some people have argued that much of history has been about the oppression of one group by another. Men have oppressed women, white people have oppressed black, the rich have oppressed the poor, and so on.

In the Bible the Book of Exodus tells how the Jews were for many years enslaved by the pharaoh (ruler) of Egypt. Jews remember this event during Passover, when they eat bitter herbs and flat bread, which they call "the bread of oppression."

For centuries people have thought that oppression was simply a fact of life. In ancient Greece and Rome, for example, people thought that the slavery endured by some was necessary for the well-being of the free.

Ordinary people expected life to be very hard even when they were not slaves. During the Middle Ages (A.D. 500–1500) the peasants (farm laborers) in the villages of Europe were told by their priests that kings and other noblemen were born to rule over them. This was God's order, the priests said.

Economic Oppression

In the 18th century thinkers began to question the idea that oppression was somehow natural or God-given. Many countries abolished legal slavery and began to move toward democracy.

Oppression, however, took on new and often less obvious forms. The first factories were built in Europe at the end of the 18th century during what was called the industrial revolution. The factory workers, who included children, were often poorly paid and ill treated by the factory owners. Later the workers formed unions to fight against this economic oppression.

Economic oppression still occurs in places in which jobs are scarce and workers' rights are few. And in some parts of the world, such as India and South America, child labor still exists. Many of the world's poor have little choice but a life of oppression.

The German political thinker Karl Marx (1818–1883) defined oppression as the domination of one social class by another. He predicted that the oppressed classes of the world—the working classes—would achieve freedom only through violent revolution.

Oppression Today

There are still many countries today where a small and sometimes very rich ruling class (elite) holds power over an oppressed majority. Myanmar (Burma), for example, is a one-party state in which free speech and political opposition are ruthlessly suppressed.

Sometimes one country oppresses another. China, for example, has occupied the formerly independent country of Tibet since 1951. The Chinese authorities make it difficult for the Tibetan people to practice their religion—a form of Buddhism—freely.

Oppression is not only carried out by governments. An oppressor can be anyone who makes somebody else's life miserable. We might, for instance, describe a school bully, a gang leader, or a tyrannical boss at work as an oppressor.

These people are demonstrating against political oppression in Chile. The banner reads: "Immediate and unconditional freedom for all political prisoners."

Oppression sometimes occurs in the home, too. Thousands of women and children in the United States, for example, live in fear in households that are dominated by violent and oppressive men. In many cities there are victim-support groups and refuges (safe places) for women and children fleeing from domestic violence.

The Motives for Oppression

The reasons why people oppress others are complicated. For some it may be a way of "getting even." Studies show that many parents who abuse their children were themselves abused as children. Psychologists say that abusers often think of themselves as righting the wrongs that were done to them in the past.

Some people have argued, however, that people learn and grow powerful from being oppressed. The German thinker Friedrich Nietzsche (1844–1900) said that "whatever does not kill me makes me stronger."

In the Bible Moses eventually rescues the Jewish people from slavery in Egypt and leads them to freedom in Israel. The long and difficult journey of the Jews to the "Promised Land" reminds us that freedom from oppression is not easily gained and that the struggle for human rights is far from over.

SEE ALSO: ABUSE, CLASS, DISCRIMINATION, FEMINISM, MINORITIES, PREJUDICE, RACISM, RIGHTS, SEXISM, TOLERANCE.

Pacifism

The term "pacifism" means the refusal to use violence as a way of resolving conflict. The term comes from the Latin word "*pax*," meaning "peace."

Seeking a Nonviolent Approach

Pacifists are people who believe that any use of violence against another human being is evil. Pacifists seek nonviolent ways to deal with conflict, particularly in times of war. A pacifist is one who adopts a peaceful or calm approach to life.

Is there any time when it is ethical to harm or kill another person? While most people agree that murder is generally wrong, some say that there are certain circumstances in which killing other humans is justified.

Many people believe that killing another person in self-defense is justified. Many people would also say that defending one's country against foreign attack or invasion is right, even if this means killing others.

Pacifism and Passivity

Some pacifists call themselves conscientious objectors—that is, people who believe that all war or a particular war is evil. Conscientious objectors refuse to join the military, even if they are drafted, except as part of a medical corps to care for the wounded.

We should not confuse "pacifism" with "passivity." Being passive means not doing anything. Pacifists are not passive when faced with violence; they often take firm action to oppose what they consider to be evil.

One pacifist response, for instance, is to commit acts of civil disobedience. During the Vietnam War (1954–1975), for example,

The Indian nationalist leader Mahatma Gandhi used pacifist methods in his campaign against British rule in India.

many young people in the United States who objected to the war protested by marching in the streets or by refusing to register for the military draft. Others became conscientious objectors. Some but not all were pacifist.

Early Christians were pacifists. Jesus said we should love our enemies, and early Christians interpreted this to mean humans should not take another life. Early Christians also refused to join the Roman army because then they would have to worship the emperor's gods. Some Christian groups remain pacifists today, such as the Society of Friends (Quakers), the Amish, and Jehovah's Witnesses.

How Far Does a Pacifist Go?

How far should pacifists go in protesting against violence? Can they work in a defense plant that makes weapons of war? Can they buy goods from a company that also makes tanks? Many pacifists believe that they are ethically bound to avoid all cooperation with governments or companies that profit from war or defense.

Should the pacifist philosophy of nonviolence apply only to human life or should it include all living creatures? In many Eastern religions there is a long tradition of reverence for all life. In Hinduism, Buddhism, and Jainism, for instance, a pacifist or nonviolent attitude toward all life is expressed in the notion of *ahisma*. *Ahisma* is a Sanskrit word that means "no harm."

Hindus believe that we are all reborn after we die and that our thoughts and actions in this life affect our next life. This is the notion of *karma*. They believe that violence has negative consequences not only in this life but also in the next.

In Jain teachings, which take *ahisma* more literally than either Hinduism or Buddhism, people must not harm any living thing, including vegetables. A Jain will wear a mask over his face, for example, to avoid breathing in an insect and will try to avoid stepping on any creature. While Jains do eat vegetables, they choose only those thought to have the least amount of life in them. However, some Jains argue that *ahisma* should mean that we eat no living thing—that we starve to death.

Gandhi's Pacifism

Mahatma Gandhi (1869–1948), who led India to independence from Britain in 1947, was influenced by the notion of *ahisma*. He employed what he called *satyagraha*, which means "truth or soul force." Soul force means returning good for evil until those who practice evil tire of doing it.

Gandhi opposed the idea of a revolutionary war to gain independence. He believed violence only blinded people with fury. Instead, he used acts of civil disobedience—general strikes, refusing to register as required by law, going to jail rather than cooperating with government leaders, and going on hunger fasts—to protest against British imperialist policies. Gandhi was willing to become a martyr if it would allow others to become free.

Martin Luther King Jr.

The civil-rights leader Martin Luther King Jr. (1929–1968) sought to end discrimination and violence against African Americans. Like Gandhi, King believed that pacifist methods were the only moral way to confront hostile and violent enemies.

He led strikes against businesses that refused to hire African-American workers and against bus companies that made African Americans sit in the rear sections of buses. King was awarded the Nobel Peace Prize in 1964 in recognition of his work in the civil-rights movement.

SEE ALSO: PROTEST, RIGHTS, VIOLENCE, WAR.

Parenting

People generally use the term "parenting" to mean "bringing up children." The term can also mean "becoming a parent," which includes such medical issues as surrogacy or in vitro fertilization (IVF).

The Right to Parenthood

For most people becoming a parent is only too easy. Human sexual impulses are strong, and in the heat of the moment it is easy to forget that parenthood will change lives and will mean serious duties and responsibilities. The very ease with which people can produce children raises a number of important ethical questions.

Many people claim that the greatest threat to humankind is overpopulation. The Western world already uses more than its fair share of the Earth's resources. If this is so, is it right to produce more children?

Having children is expensive. Potential parents must ask themselves whether they are earning enough to meet this expense or whether they will simply expect the state to pay. Children are also expensive in time and attention. Are people willing to give up other things in the interests of their children?

They also have to ask themselves whether their relationship is stable and permanent. If not, is it right to impose all the burdens on one person, usually the woman? Should a child be deprived of role models of both sexes? Have they considered the effects on children of one-parent families?

In an ideal world people would discuss these and other questions about parenting early in their relationship, before they start having sex. In the real world, though, this rarely happens. Often people discover they are expecting a baby before they have thought through these issues for themselves, let alone discussed them with their partner.

Questions about parenting involve moral issues that affect the rights of individuals. We cannot claim to be ethical if we are concerned only with our own satisfaction and ignore the possibility that we may be infringing the rights of others.

The Rights of Children

Babies are not born with a built-in system of ethics. Their view of the world is, at first, entirely one-sided and concerned only with meeting their own needs. It is not long, however, before small children discover that other people have needs and that some kind of compromise is necessary.

Finding a satisfactory solution to this problem—meeting everyone's needs—is one of the most important aspects of growing up into a mature and socially responsible citizen. Parents have a duty to ensure that children find the right solution.

To a small child parents are all-knowing and all-powerful. At least for a time the child accepts the parents' views and opinions as true. This can have good or bad consequences, depending on the parents' values.

Children respond well to secure affection and love, especially from the parent who cares for them every day. Being loved and cared for helps children learn about the needs and rights of others.

People who have been denied affection as children often lack empathy. They cannot put themselves in the place of others and

Although many children in the U.S. grow up in single-parent families, the traditional family of parents and their children is still the norm. This family group spans three generations.

consider others' feelings. Studies have shown that lack of empathy can lead to delinquent and criminal behavior.

As the child begins to learn to speak, what the parents say to him becomes very important and can have a life-long influence for good or ill. If the parents encourage the child and praise him for good behavior, he is likely to grow up feeling secure and loved and have high self-esteem. If, however, they mostly criticize him and rarely praise him, he is likely to grow up feeling insecure and

lacking in confidence. If few of his own needs for love and care are met, he is also less likely to consider others' needs as important.

Much of a child's character is formed by the time she is about seven, so the responsibility on parents is a large one. In many cases adults are not aware of the power and responsibility they have to influence their children until it is too late. For this reason many people argue that a society that ignores the importance of educating its young people for parenting has failed them.

Ethics and Infertility

For infertile people who would like to have children, other ethical questions arise. Such people are usually in a stable relationship and, in many cases, are able to afford to have children and to provide them with the care all children need.

If natural methods do not work, some people try to have a child by artificially fertilizing the woman's egg. This procedure occurs in a laboratory and is called in vitro fertilization (IVF). Couples can also try to adopt a child.

Failing this, infertile couples may consider surrogacy. This means another woman (the surrogate mother) has the baby and

hands it over after the birth. Sometimes the surrogate mother's egg is artificially fertilized by the male partner's sperm. If the man is infertile, the sperm may come from an anonymous donor. In some cases fertilization takes place in the laboratory using eggs and sperm from the couple, and the embryo is implanted in the surrogate mother's womb.

Surrogacy raises important ethical problems. Carrying a baby in the womb for nine months creates a strong emotional bond between mother and child. The mother's distress when the baby is handed over can be extreme. Is this fair to the surrogate mother? Should she be paid a large sum of money for her services? Are those who seek surrogacy exploiting a fellow human being for their own advantage? Should the surrogate mother be anonymous or known to the couple? Is surrogacy justified if the surrogate mother is a close relative? Should the child be told about his or her surrogate mother?

In some cases women have been paid large sums of money to be surrogate mothers. Once they are pregnant, though, some feel that they want to keep the baby. In one case, at least, the surrogate mother pretended she had had an abortion because she could not face handing over the baby.

Cases such as these arouse fierce controversy. Some people believe surrogacy is just another aspect of our consumerist society. Others believe that women should have the right to have their own children by any means. Many people admit that it is difficult, if not impossible, to work out an ethical system for surrogacy that does not deny someone his or her rights.

The IVF procedure, in which eggs are fertilized in a laboratory, helps previously childless couples become parents.

Single-Parent Families

Today single-parent families account for at least a quarter of all families in the United States. People's attitudes toward the family have changed since the 1970s, and they are more likely to accept single-parent families as a fact of life.

Many people, however, believe that it is best for children to be brought up by parents of both sexes. About 90 percent of single parents are women, and some people are concerned that children are growing up without male role models.

Single parents usually cannot work and look after their children at the same time. Either they must be unemployed or—if another family member cannot help out—pay someone to look after their children. In some cases single parents have to rely on the welfare system to pay for their childcare.

Some people believe that single-parent families contribute to social problems, such as crime and delinquency. Studies have shown, for example, that delinquent children often come from single-parent families.

The reasons for the growth in single-parent families are many. They include the greater acceptance of divorce, women's desire for independence from men and their wish to fulfill themselves in employment, changing attitudes to sex, greater tolerance of mothers being unmarried, more liberal attitudes to what used to be called illegitimacy (when children are born to parents who are not married), and a decline in the belief that marriage has a religious basis.

Who Should Have Children?

Does everyone have the right to have children? Are we entitled to try to restrict women in poor countries from having babies for economic reasons? Is a woman who is long past the normal reproductive age entitled to have a baby, now that this is medically possible? In China the policy is that families should have only one child. Are the authorities justified in punishing couples who have more than one child? There are no easy answers to these questions.

SEE ALSO: ABORTION, CHILD ABUSE, FAMILY, FEMINISM, MARRIAGE, MEDICAL ETHICS, MONOGAMY, RELATIONSHIPS, SEXUAL BEHAVIOR.

EUGENICS

In the past various authorities have decided that there are classes of people who should not be allowed to become parents. The study of the "improvement" of a race or population by selective breeding is called eugenics.

In positive eugenics people considered to be of good genetic stock are encouraged to have children. In negative eugenics people thought to be of inferior stock are prevented from having children or are even forcibly sterilized (made infertile).

Negative eugenics was widespread in the United States, Canada, and Europe until well into the 20th century. In Sweden, for instance, some 60,000 people were forcibly sterilized for eugenic reasons from the 1930s until the 1970s. In many cases the grounds for their sterilization were "undesirable racial characteristics," some of which are now known not to be inheritable. Many U.S. states also passed laws allowing eugenics to be practiced.

Similar policies were followed by the Nazi government in Germany (1933–1945). The Nazis believed that the Aryan race was being "polluted" by foreign influences. They followed a policy of "eliminating" those they considered to be racially inferior.

Patriotism

A country's flag is a powerful focus of patriotism, and flying the national flag is one way that people express their love of or devotion to their country.

The term "patriotism" generally refers to love of or devotion to one's own country and the desire to preserve its institutions, culture, and distinct way of life.

Willingness to Fight

Anyone who supports the country in which he or she lives is a patriot to some degree. Many people believe patriotism means being willing to go to war and, if necessary, to die to protect one's homeland. However, people who consider themselves "true" patriots often suspect their fellow countrymen and women—and on occasion their own government—of being unpatriotic because these people do not share their own views on what patriotism means.

For some people patriotism can be summed up by part of a toast proposed at a banquet in Virginia by U.S. Navy officer Stephen Decatur in 1816: "…my country, right or wrong." What Decatur meant was that he was willing to support his country without exception even if the reasons for its leaders' actions were unlawful or morally dubious. Many patriots would agree with him.

Is Patriotism for Scoundrels?

At the other extreme are those who view patriotism as "the last refuge of the scoundrel." This saying, coined by English writer Dr. Samuel Johnson (1709–1784), suggests that some people use patriotism to justify their sometimes morally dubious actions. They rely on the emotional pull that patriotism has for many people.

Most people would say that their feelings about patriotism fall somewhere between these two extremes. Often, though, it is difficult to identify the point at which patriotism becomes so extreme that it is used to justify morally unacceptable actions.

Defending the Country

In time of crisis governments often "play the patriotic card." If they are threatened by a foreign power, for instance, they may argue that it is the patriotic duty of their citizens to fight in their country's defense.

Depending on how open and democratic the society is, the mass media—radio, television, and newspapers—either follow the government's line or are prevented from reporting news or discussing issues that might damage the government's position.

Sometimes this rallying cry to defend one's country is justified, but not always. If our homeland is invaded by a foreign power, most of us would agree that it is our patriotic duty to fight back. If, however, our country goes to war to conquer a neighboring territory, many people would find it difficult to justify taking part.

Some people argue that an emotional call on citizens to do their patriotic duty is a way for a government to avoid a full discussion of the issues that have led to war. They point out that a government that can explain its reasons for going to war in a clear, unemotional way—not by appealing to people's patriotic feelings—is more likely to win the long-term support of its citizens (especially those who will have to fight).

Objections to War

In undemocratic countries governments expect and demand patriotism. In its most extreme form patriotism can become aggressive nationalism and fascism. Under such regimes people are always expected to be patriotic and wholly supportive of the government. If they refuse, they might be imprisoned or even face execution.

In democratic countries governments may have a right to expect their citizens to be patriotic, but they cannot demand their patriotism. Even in democratic countries, though, people who refuse to fight in wartime because of their strong antiwar beliefs can be punished and even imprisoned.

Some people, for example, may hold religious or moral beliefs against taking life and refuse to go to war in any circumstances. Some patriots would argue that people who refuse to fight (conscientious objectors) are siding with the enemy and are acting in an unpatriotic or treacherous way.

Other people may hold antiwar views but only about a particular conflict. Some people objected to the U.S. involvement in the Vietnam War (1954–1975), for example. They felt that the U.S. government's interference in the conflict was not justified.

Although many people saw the antiwar movement as unpatriotic, some of the protesters argued that they were the true patriots and that it was the U.S. government that was acting immorally.

SEE ALSO: CITIZENSHIP, DEMOCRACY, FASCISM, NATIONALISM, PACIFISM, PROTEST, WAR.

Peer Pressure

Our peers are those with whom we are in some way equal. Peer pressure is a psychological or social force that people in the same peer group exert on one another, whether intentionally or not.

Peer Groups

Usually, our peers are similar in age to us, live in the same or similar communities, and go to the same schools. Our peers do not have to be our friends—in fact, we may not even know them personally—but they are like us in various ways.

When individuals say or do certain things to be like their peers, we describe their behavior as being influenced by peer pressure. For example, when certain members of a group adopt a particular hairstyle (such as a shaven head) or dress code (torn blue jeans), other members may change their hair or clothes to fit in with the group.

As more and more members of the group shave their heads or start wearing torn jeans, it becomes increasingly difficult for others in the group to resist the pressure to fit in, or conform.

Many of the things we do in our everyday lives result from peer pressure of one form or another. However, no one usually sets out to make others wear their hair or

We all want to have a sense of belonging, but sometimes peer pressure can cause us to act first and think later.

clothes in a particular way. And those people who do respond to peer pressure do not always do so consciously. In fact, one of the problems with peer pressure is that it can lead people to do harmful things—either to themselves or others—without thinking.

For instance, some gang members may carry guns or knives or take drugs so that they can remain part of the gang. Even if they question whether this is right or wrong, they may feel they have little choice if they do not want to be left out.

The Desire to Belong

Peer pressure can be a problem even when people are fully aware that they are behaving in a certain way only because that is what

their peers are doing. A person might agree that his behavior or appearance is being influenced by peer pressure, but he might still feel that he has no real choice—he just wants to fit in. Even if he did not want to behave or dress in that way, his desire, or need, to fit in is stronger than his desire to be an individual and think for himself.

Identity and Peer Pressure

Among young people peer pressure often operates on the surface, influencing what we wear and what we do. This, in itself, can be a problem because it encourages individuals to copy one another on a surface (superficial) level rather than ask themselves what is right or appropriate in a particular situation.

Because peer pressure tends to make people conform, it discourages individuals from "being themselves"—from expressing their own unique personality. It can even discourage people from taking up certain pursuits, such as playing a musical instrument, or performing well at school if the group does not place a value on these skills.

Most people need to feel that they belong to something or someone. For a young child being a loved member of a family might be the most important thing. One of the key features of adolescence, however, is the need to find one's own identity. Often this means finding, or searching for, a group outside the family to which to belong.

Our peers also influence what we believe and value or, at least, what we are prepared to say we believe and value. People who are particularly vulnerable to peer pressure may believe that they are thinking for themselves because they hold beliefs that are different from those of their family. In reality, though, they are simply conforming all over again, this time to their peer group.

The Value of Conformity

Not all peer pressure is negative or creates problems. There are many reasons why most people obey the law and generally behave in a peaceful and sociable manner. Peer pressure is one such reason: most people do not want to be singled out and punished by those in authority, so they tend to conform to what society expects of them.

There is nothing noble or virtuous about behaving differently from others just for the sake of it. Equally, however, we should not simply copy what others do just for the sake of it. What we should try to do—and it is not always easy—is to think for ourselves and decide when it is appropriate to follow our peers and when it is not. In other words, we should try to resist peer pressure when it begins to interfere with the way we think and make decisions.

Peer pressure is usually very strong in schools. Although it can sometimes distort our judgment about the right thing to do, at other times peer pressure can be positive. If, for example, the "leaders" of a peer group can be encouraged to think for themselves, then others in the group may also start to think for themselves so as to be seen as belonging to the group.

It is unrealistic to think that we could ever totally resist peer pressure: the desire to fit in is just too great in many situations. However, it is important for us to think for ourselves in all cases. Then we will be more aware of the reasons behind the things we say and do. We will be more likely to strike a balance between unthinking conformity and simply trying to be "different."

SEE ALSO: BELIEF, BULLYING, CONFORMITY, DELINQUENCY, DRUG ABUSE, GANGS, GOSSIP, IDENTITY, SECRECY, VALUES.

Person

What is a person? And what is the difference between a person and a human being? Philosophers have long pondered these kinds of question. In general, however, we might suggest that ethically speaking, a person is a human being who has moral rights and duties.

Becoming a Person

Not all human beings have full moral rights and duties. Some people would argue that a fetus in the womb has rights, but no one would argue that it has any duties. A fetus is not capable of independent thought or action and therefore can have no responsibility. We would probably say, then, that a fetus is not yet a person, though we would say that it has the potential to be one.

So when does a human being become a person? Many of us would probably answer, "When he or she is born." In this instance we are likely to find ourselves on firmer ground. While many people would think that it is regrettable but sometimes necessary— because of reasons of emotional or physical health—for a woman to have an abortion, few would approve of the murder of an infant (infanticide) on similar grounds.

Certainly, we usually think of a baby as having more rights than a fetus. But does a baby have duties? We would probably think that it does not. A baby, after all, is still helpless, dependent on its parents, and can make no moral decisions.

Nevertheless, we probably feel that a baby is well on its way to becoming a person. It is developing a consciousness (awareness) of the world and other people and of the

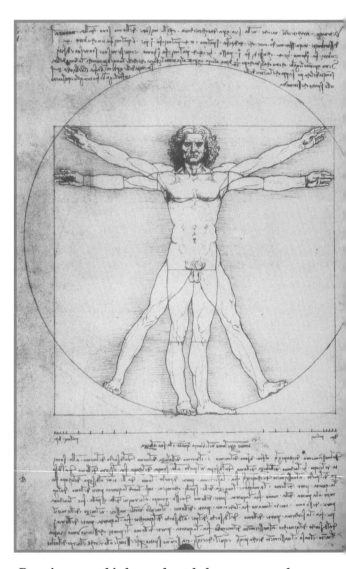

Renaissance thinkers placed the person—the individual as a legal and moral being—center stage. This drawing by Italian artist Leonardo da Vinci illustrates the idea that "Man [a person] is the measure of all things."

relationship between itself and them. Our uncertainty about whether a newborn is a person or not is reflected in the way that we sometimes refer to a baby as "it," not as "he" or "she." It is as if we feel that babies are too young to be thought of as gendered persons.

Learning a Role

Perhaps we could argue that a human being learns to become a person as he or she grows older and matures intellectually and physically. This takes us back to the roots of the word, the Latin *persona*, which referred to a character or role in a play. In a very real sense we learn to take on the role of a moral being.

Throughout childhood we gradually understand more and more about how our actions affect other people and the world in which we live. And at the same time, we learn how the actions of other people and our society can affect us.

We have an increasing sense of our responsibilities and of the rights that are our due. In this sense we could say that we never stop becoming a person, even after we have legally reached adulthood. We are always learning to become moral beings.

Persons and the Law

Usually, we find that this idea of personhood is reflected in the law. For example, societies generally give more legal rights and duties to an adult than to a child. An adult has the right to vote, to marry, and to drive a car; she also a duty to pay taxes and is held to be legally responsible if she commits a crime.

A child, on the other hand, does not have any of these rights and duties, although sometimes she is held to be responsible to a degree for a delinquent or criminal act.

In this way we can see how the idea of personhood ties in with that of citizenship. An important part of becoming a person is becoming a citizen—taking on our rights and duties as a member of society.

Persons and the Right to Life

Many societies past and present have denied personhood to some human beings. They have considered them in some way to be "non-persons." In ancient Athens, for example, slaves were entirely without legal rights and could be bought, sold, or even killed by their masters. And in Nazi Germany (1933–1945) the government deprived Jews of their citizenship, personhood, and finally their lives.

From these examples we can see how the idea of personhood is very often closely related to the right to life. Once a human being is no longer recognized as a person, it becomes much easier to deny him his rights altogether, including his right to life.

Take, for instance, the example of someone who has become permanently unconscious after a road accident. Does her condition make her less of a person? Does she no longer have any rights? And does her doctor have the right to switch off her life-support system?

These are difficult questions to answer. The accident victim can no longer be said to have any duties to those around her. But are we therefore justified in denying her any rights? Some would argue that the fact that she was once an individual with rights and responsibilities must count for something.

And what about those people with severe learning difficulties? They neither have been full moral beings nor can they ever become so. Our society tends to treat such people as "less-than-persons," denying them, for example, the right to vote or to have children. Some people would argue that our definition of personhood ought to be expanded to include all human beings.

SEE ALSO: ABORTION, CITIZENSHIP, DUTY, ETHICS, EUTHANASIA, HUMANISM, IDENTITY, INDEPENDENCE, LAW, RESPONSIBILITY, RIGHTS.

Pity

When we feel sorrow for the suffering of another, we feel pity for him. Pity is an altruistic emotion; it means we are thinking about others' needs and interests.

A Christian Virtue

The words "pity," "pious," and "piety" all come from the Latin word "*pius*," which means "pious" or "dutiful." In many ways it is our duty to take pity on the suffering of others. Without pity we remain unmoved by others' pain, ignorant of their suffering.

In the Christian tradition pity has been seen as an important virtue. In Christian religious artworks it has often been represented in images of the Virgin Mary mourning over the body of Christ. Such images are entitled "Pietà," which is the Italian word for "pity."

Caring for Others

Pity is similar to sympathy, compassion, and empathy but is not the same. Sympathy, compassion, and empathy involve sharing the other person's suffering. When we feel empathy for someone else, we feel what the other person is feeling.

Today, though, we generally do not value pity as highly as we once did. Unlike sympathy, compassion, or empathy, pity frequently has a negative meaning. When we feel pity for someone, we hold ourselves at a distance from the person who is suffering. We view his suffering as something that makes him different from us.

In contrast, when we feel compassion for someone rather than pity, we recognize that we are capable of suffering in the same way.

In other words, we recognize that there is a shared humanity between us and the person for whom we feel compassion.

"I Don't Want Your Pity"

While we want others to have sympathy or compassion for our situation, we often do not want them to pity us. Feeling pity implies that those who feel pity are in some way superior to those they are pitying. We often hear people say, "I don't want your pity!" When someone pities us, we recognize that although she feels sorrow for us, in an important way she is also looking down on us.

Similarly, when we feel pity for ourselves—when we feel self-pity—we see ourselves as objects to be pitied. Self-pity is a negative emotion. It means we are putting ourselves in a lower position relative to others and asking others to do the same. When we feel self-pity, we feel we have little or no power to relieve our suffering.

Why Do We Feel Pity?

Sometimes we feel pity rather than compassion or empathy for another's suffering because we think that person has in some way brought the suffering on himself or that he deserved it. We are sorry for him and feel regret at his misfortune, but we do not necessarily have fellow feeling for him.

At other times we feel pity when we know that the person who is suffering has no control over his situation. We may feel pity, for instance, for someone who has had an accident that has left him with disabilities. However, it is possible to feel both compassion and pity for someone.

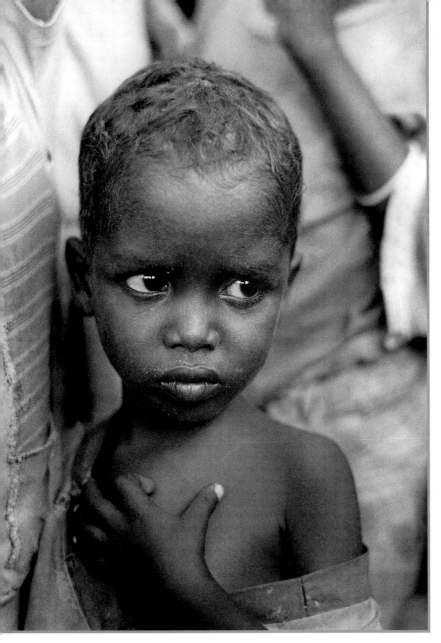

Images such as this one of a hungry child in Somalia often cause us to feel pity for the suffering of others. Aid agencies use such images to make us think about what we can do to help relieve the suffering of other people.

to ease our consciences, but compassion urges us to take action that is more long-lasting. Pity usually does not move us in the same way that compassion does.

On television and in magazines and newspapers in the West we see numerous and often shocking images of the suffering of others elsewhere in the world. Many of us in the Western world live in comfort with plenty to eat, while others have been forced from their homes or are starving. Such images may play on our guilt about our comfortable lives.

International aid agencies often use these images of others' suffering to prick our consciences. When we feel pity, it is hard for us to sit back and do nothing. We may feel moved to donate a few dollars to help the needy. If we feel compassionate, on the other hand, we may want to do more, such as volunteer to work for the charity that is providing aid.

Sometimes pity becomes compassion once we understand more about a person's situation. If, for instance, we find out that a person was abused as a child or that she lost her parents when she was very young, we are likely to feel compassion rather than simply pity.

Spurs to Action

Another important difference between pity and compassion is that when we feel compassion, we are more likely to take action than if we feel pity. Pity may make us want

SEE ALSO: ALTRUISM, CHARITY, COMPASSION, CONSCIENCE, CRUELTY, EGOISM, EMOTIONS, EMPATHY, GUILT, HATE, LOVE, OPPRESSION, POVERTY, SUFFERING, TOLERANCE.

Political Conduct

The term "political conduct" refers to the way politicians behave when they are doing their jobs. In general we use the term to refer not so much to how well they do their work in politics but rather to the extent to which their actions and behavior in political life are ethical.

Honest Politicians

It is part of the stock-in-trade of many comics to make jokes about the ethical standards of politicians. "Here lies a politician and an honest man," quotes the humorist, then, after a pause, adds: "What, two men in one grave?" This is typical of the rather cynical attitude many people have toward professional politicians.

There is, however, a serious point behind the humor. The British politician Lord Acton (1834–1902) might be forgotten today but for a remark he made in a letter to the editor of the *English Historical Review:* "Power tends to corrupt," he said, "and absolute power corrupts absolutely." This saying has

President Richard Nixon (right) resigned from office in 1974 after it was discovered he had used illegal methods in his 1972 reelection campaign.

become well known. It is because power tends to corrupt that we expect very high standards from politicians—higher standards than from people in other walks of life.

The history of political power in the 20th century shows us how easy it is for absolute political power to lead to serious corruption. The 20th century was dominated by figures such as Joseph Stalin (1879–1953), Adolf Hitler (1889–1945), Benito Mussolini (1883–1945), and Mao Tse-tung (1893–1976). They were all ruthless dictators and in some cases were guilty of very cruel acts and evil-doing.

The Appeal of Politics

People who enter politics usually want to make a difference to the way a country is governed. And making a difference to a country's government usually involves getting into political office.

In turn, political office at any level offers people power over others: power to help and please as well as power to harm and oppress. Politics provides office-holders with status and the opportunity to do favors. It commands obedience and, in some cases, respect.

There are all kinds of ways in which people in positions of power can obtain financial and other personal advantages. And if politicians as a group enjoy less respect than they think is due to them, it is because they have, often in minor ways, abused their power.

Consider, for instance, the question of the funding of political parties. Political campaigning is expensive, often costing millions of dollars. Where is this money to come from? In almost all cases there will be large single contributions from wealthy individuals and business corporations.

In most cases people would not make donations unless they believed an advantage would follow. So candidates must either repay the contributors by providing some favor or avoid doing so and lose the support of the donors. In the first instance they are virtually selling favors; in the second they are guilty of ingratitude.

Since both alternatives involve unethical behavior, some people argue that it is wrong to accept large single donations for campaign funds. This point is often ignored, though, and donors are even praised for making such donations.

SEE ALSO: ABUSE, CITIZENSHIP, CONDUCT, CORRUPTION, DEMOCRACY, POWER.

THE PRIVATE LIVES OF POLITICIANS

To what extent should politicians, as public figures, be considered as role models for the general population? Most people think that politicians should try to set an example to others, and everyone would agree that public behavior must be beyond reproach.

But some people argue that a person's private behavior, especially sexual behavior, is a matter for him or her alone. Is there any real difference between public and private behavior, though? Consider the case of a married politician who has sexual relationships (affairs) with other people. Some would argue that a person who cheats on his or her spouse is dishonest and should be disqualified from public office.

Others say we can have different rules for different situations. Attitudes change over time, too. In Britain in the 1960s the politician John Profumo was forced to resign from politics after admitting he had been having an affair. Today the majority of the American public appears to accept that a president of the United States can have sexual activity outside marriage without losing much popularity or even credibility.

Pornography

Many cities have laws that bookstores and theaters offering pornography must be located on the outskirts of the city or at a certain distance from schools and residential neighborhoods.

The depiction of sexual acts in any media (writing, artworks, movies, photography, and so on) that is intended to arouse sexual excitement is called pornography.

Pornography and Erotica

Not all writings or pictures with sexual, or erotic, content are meant to arouse sexual excitement in those who view them. They are not therefore considered to be pornographic. The Bible, for example, has many erotic passages, but most people would not consider these to be pornographic.

Some of the greatest works of visual art in almost every age have depicted the nude human body, and many of these have depicted sexual situations or acts. In most of these cases, however, the feelings the artist aroused in the viewer are aesthetic (having to do with beauty) rather than sexual. Sometimes, however, a writer or artist may intend her work to arouse both aesthetic and sexual feelings, and her work may count both as great art and pornography.

No one who produces erotic material can prevent that material from being used by someone else for the purpose of sexual arousal. Some readers, for example, find fashion magazines—in which models are usually fully clothed—sexually stimulating. This, however, does not make these magazines pornographic. Some people argue that it is the intent of the person who creates the material to cause sexual arousal, not the intent of the person who uses the material, that makes the material pornographic.

Pornography and Obscenity

"Obscenity" is a term used by lawmakers to define what kinds of pornography it is illegal to make or use. We call this process of deciding the legality of published materials "censorship." Most censorship laws try to ban only those materials that would offend "the average person" or a large number of people in a community.

Not all erotic or even all pornographic material is obscene, and not all obscene material is erotic or pornographic. Advertisers, for example, commonly use sexual words and images to sell products. While some of this material is offensive to some people, most of it is not so offensive that it would meet the legal definition of obscenity.

Material that is considered obscene in one culture may not be in another, and all cultures change their standards of decency over time. What today we would consider modest, such as images of people in bathing suits or people kissing, has been thought obscene in certain times and places.

Does Pornography Cause Crime?

Some people believe that all pornography is immoral because it is an inappropriate way for people to use sexuality. They believe that the proper use of sexuality is limited, by God or by nature, to procreation (producing children) and the expression of love between married heterosexual (different-sex) couples.

Other people believe that making or viewing pornography is not immoral in itself, but that doing so can lead to criminal behavior, such as rape or child abuse.

It would be wrong, however, to argue that pornography is a necessary cause of sexual crime or that without it there would be no sexual crime. If, say, a rapist used pornography, we could argue that his sexual attitudes led to both his interest in pornography and his crimes. We cannot assume that it was pornography that caused his crimes. And, of course, the vast majority of pornography users do not commit sexual crimes.

Pornography, Democracy, and Harm

Most people believe that in a democracy the law should only be used to stop people from harming each other, not to prevent certain people from doing things that other people believe to be immoral or unwise. Such people would argue, therefore, that even if we disapprove of pornography, we do not have the right to ban people from using it.

The same people would argue, however, that where pornography does cause harm, there should be laws to protect people. For instance, most societies have laws against children being involved in the making or the use of pornography, because these activities are considered to be harmful to them.

Many feminists argue that pornography can harm women, particularly when it portrays them as being merely sexual objects. Pornography, they say, can contribute to a sexist view of women because in most pornography sex is depicted as something that women always do for the pleasure of men. Images that present unequal sexual roles can strengthen other, nonsexual inequalities between men and women, they argue.

Many people believe there is nothing immoral about making or using pornography, as long as no one is harmed. These people point out that moderate use of pornography can help improve loving relationships between sexual partners.

SEE ALSO: ABUSE, CENSORSHIP, CHILD ABUSE, ETHICS, FEMINISM, MEDIA, SEXISM, SEXUAL BEHAVIOR, SPEECH, VIOLENCE.

Poverty

"For ye have the poor always with you."
MATTHEW 26.11

When people are unable to support themselves or their family—that is, when they cannot afford, or have no access to, adequate shelter, food, or health care—we say that they are living in poverty.

Some people, however, go further and argue that we can describe as poor even those people who do have enough to live on (subsist) but who are considerably less well off than most other people in their society.

The first definition of poverty is sometimes called "absolute poverty," while the second is called "relative poverty."

Poverty amid Plenty

Few people would argue with the fact that today the United States, like other Western nations, is a society of plenty; that is, it is a society that has enough wealth to meet far more than its citizens' subsistence needs.

But there is poverty in U.S. society, too. While this poverty is rarely of the absolute kind—few people could be said to be starving—many people live in relative poverty. Such people have a very low quality of life and have inadequate access to education, health care, and employment.

In some towns or cities we have probably noticed how extreme wealth and poverty can exist side by side. Although U.S. society as a whole is rich, its wealth is very unevenly distributed. In the United States about 45 percent of the income is concentrated in the hands of 20 percent of the population. Wealth is also unevenly distributed among the sexes and ethnic groups: women are much poorer than men, and African Americans are poorer than white Americans.

Many people believe that this huge—and some would say widening—gulf between rich and poor calls into question the whole moral fabric of Western societies.

Poverty and Charity

The vast majority of us feel compassion for the poor. We have all probably felt a nagging sense of guilt when we walk past a homeless person in the street on our way to buy a pair of sneakers that we do not really need.

But most people would argue, too, that to be truly compassionate, we need to do more than feel guilt and pity, and that it is our duty to intervene actively in some way.

The traditional response has always been charity—the giving of money or goods to people in need. There are, however, a number of problems with charity as a means of relieving poverty.

In small-scale societies charity was often a sure way of helping those in need. In close-knit communities everyone knew everyone, and it was obvious when someone had fallen on hard times. In a complex, large-scale society such as the United States, by contrast, we know few people outside our immediate circle of friends and family, and as a result others' poverty is largely hidden from us.

Most of us do not know what it is like to be very poor. If we do give to the poor, it is often because we have come across poverty only by chance. We might, for example, see a homeless person on the street, feel sorry for him, and give him some money.

Holy men and women sometimes show their disregard for material things by taking vows of poverty and living by the charity of others. Here a young Buddhist monk receives alms outside a temple in Bangkok, Thailand.

Poverty and Welfare

Liberal democracies have generally tried to tackle poverty by setting up a system of benefits to act as a "safety net." If someone is unable to earn her own income—whether because of unemployment, sickness, or old age—she can fall back on government benefits to prevent the worst effects of poverty.

Welfare replaces the insecurity of charity with the security of benefits. No one is left at the mercy of someone else's charity. Others argue, too, that welfare helps ease the stigma (negative image) of poverty by making freedom from want a citizen's right.

On the other hand, some people argue that welfare deepens the gulf between rich and poor—between a privileged class that earns an income and an underclass that is permanently dependent on benefits.

Challenging Poverty at Its Roots

Some people argue that both private charity and public welfare ignore the real roots of poverty—the unfair distribution of wealth. Both are short-term, stop-gap measures that make us feel poverty is a fact of life and that the best we can do is to help out occasionally when we see real distress.

Other people would say that poverty is not natural but "human-made." In their opinion capitalism (which is a kind of economic free-for-all) leads to some people taking more than their fair share of the available wealth.

Moreover, they say, racist and sexist attitudes in society mean that ethnic minorities and women are often at a serious disadvantage when it comes to getting a good job and making a decent wage.

Some of these critics would argue that we ought to change the economic basis of our society. Communists, for example, would argue that we should redistribute wealth by force. Critics of communism argue that the loss of personal and political freedoms that have often accompanied attempts to set up communist societies (as in the former Soviet Union and China) suggest that the price paid for economic equality is too high. Other people argue for a more moderate redistribution of wealth via a fairer taxation system and the setting of a minimum wage.

The enormous cost of welfare presents Western governments with one of the great ethical and political dilemmas of the 21st century. We will have to decide whether we want society to continue to protect its citizens from poverty, and accordingly be prepared to pay more in taxes, or whether we are to accept the biblical belief that "the poor are always with us."

Children are often the main victims of poverty. These girls live in an impoverished district, or "ghetto," of Los Angeles.

World Poverty

More than ever before we are aware of the poverty that exists worldwide. Television shows us heartbreaking images of absolute poverty—of starving children and famine refugees lying exhausted. This awareness has extended the ethical challenge of poverty: do we have a duty to help the millions of starving people worldwide, and, if so, to what lengths should we take this duty?

Some people have argued that in fact we do not have a duty to help people in other countries. For one thing, so this argument goes, it is impractical for us to give charity to those far away, especially when there are so many in need. We do better, they argue, to use our money to help those near to us because we can reasonably expect this to be effective.

Others argue that our duty to help other human beings is the same whether they are close by or far away. If we know that somewhere people are suffering, we ought to try to help them wherever they are. More than this, we ought to give as much money as we can to help those who are suffering, without making ourselves poor as a consequence.

Still others say that both these viewpoints are extreme. They argue that we need to rethink the problem. Charity, they suggest, is not the solution to world poverty. It would be better to help impoverished countries address the underlying causes of poverty (war and corruption, for example).

They also point out that more often than not it is the greed of Western societies—our consumption of more than our fair share of the Earth's resources—that condemns the rest of the world to poverty.

SEE ALSO: CAPITALISM, CHARITY, CLASS, COMMUNISM & SOCIALISM, COMPASSION, EQUALITY, GREED, PITY, SUFFERING.

Power

"Power doesn't corrupt people, people corrupt power."   WILLIAM GADDIS

The ability or capacity to act or accomplish something is called power. We can use power to control other people, just as other people can use power to control us. We can use power to do good as well as to do harm.

From Brute Force to Political Control

Power at its most basic is physical—it is brute force. Our bodies are stronger or weaker to different degrees. Generally speaking, men are stronger than women, and adults are stronger than children.

In ancient societies physical power easily became social power. Men, with their superior physical strength, were able to exert authority over women. The strongest men—those who were best able to protect their society from enemy attack or natural disaster—became leaders of their people, who had little choice but to obey.

Political power was distributed unevenly among the members of society. Usually, there was a small, powerful elite (aristocracy) who ruled a relatively powerless majority.

As societies grew bigger, such power structures became increasingly more complex. There was often a hierarchy of power relations between the different classes. Families, too, had their own power structures, typically with the eldest male in authority.

Political and social power was usually backed up by the law. The oppression of women, for example, was usually codified (set out) in laws, such as those banning women from owning or inheriting property. In many societies women were prevented from becoming rulers in their own right and could rule only through a male.

Similarly, in the southern states of the United States the social disempowerment (removal of power) of African Americans was, from the late 19th century to the 1950s, made legal by "segregation laws." These required African Americans to use separate schools and restaurants and to sit in restricted areas on buses, for example.

Some people have even argued that the law has very little to do with justice or fairness and much more to do with who has power in society. This was the viewpoint, for example, of one of the characters in *The Republic,* a work by the Greek philosopher Plato (c. 428–c. 348 B.C.). "Justice," the character proclaims, "is nothing else than the interest of the strongest."

With the development of trade and money, social and political power were joined by, and to some extent followed, economic power. In a marriage, for example, a man not only very often had legal power over his wife, he also had economic power—women were dependent on men for their livelihood.

Rights Not Might

From the 18th century many thinkers began to challenge the traditional power structures of society. New ideas about human rights and equality began to replace the ancient assumption that "might is right."

Almost every aspect of Western society came to be reassessed in the light of these new ideas. The power relations between men and women, between different races and

Is this the real face of power? Bill Gates, who runs Microsoft Inc., wields enormous power in the international community. Today a lot of political power lies with multinational corporations.

Hidden Powers

Some people have said that despite democratic rights and freedoms, our lives are largely shaped by other, hidden power structures that exist outside those of democracy. They point out, for instance, that in Western societies inequalities in economic power have remained largely intact and that this undermines political and legal equality.

In the United States, for example, African Americans have, in theory, won full legal and political equality, and yet some continue to be relatively powerless. Some people argue that this is because African Americans earn substantially less than other Americans because of prejudice and discrimination against them.

And this relative economic powerlessness, so the argument goes, all too easily becomes political and legal powerlessness. An African American found guilty of murder, for example, is far more likely to face the death penalty simply because he will probably be unable to afford an expensive lawyer.

Other people argue that the freedom of the individual is restricted by the power of multinational corporations. These super-rich organizations are able to set prices, influence the media (newspapers, radio, and television), and control the flow of money around the world.

Critics also argue that because the world's media are largely owned by a small, powerful elite, this can effectively disempower the individual, too. Ideally, in a democracy the media ought to function as a kind of noticeboard for the exchange of ideas and criticisms of those in power. But if the media put forward only a single point of view—that of the rich and powerful—the result is propaganda (persuasive strategies) and the undermining of democracy.

classes, and even between nations were redrawn in the interests of greater equality. The ideal was that political power should be carefully limited, so that no one person could have too much power. Governments were to be ruled by consent, not by force. In practice, of course, this did not always happen.

Some people would argue that the main goal of liberal democracy is to empower (give power to) the individual, but not at the expense of another's disempowerment.

Self-empowerment

Even if we disagree with some or all of these ideas, most people would probably feel that in modern life the individual can very often feel powerless and at the mercy of forces beyond his or her control. Even when we are young, we may feel that our lives have already somehow been mapped out for us and that in reality we have very little choice about what happens to us.

Some people point out that by trying to understand the power structures that govern our lives, we can begin to take some power back into our hands. Others argue, too, that we can in fact learn to shape our own lives, that we can make our own choices.

This philosophy, or ethic, is sometimes called "self-empowerment." Self-empowerment was one of the major driving forces in Western society in the second half of the 20th century. Feminism, the African-American civil-rights movement, and gay liberation, for example, were all attempts by oppressed minority groups to take power. And today there are countless "self-help" books available that are supposed to assist people in taking control of their lives.

Some people, while they support the rights of oppressed groups, are critical of the ethic of self-empowerment that has swept through Western society. They argue that it is one more expression of the excessive emphasis placed on the individual's rights in Western societies.

A Balance of Power

Many people argue that in order to live together successfully in a society, we have to accept that there are going to be some power structures. Imagine what would happen in a family, for example, if no one made any decisions or laid down any rules.

At the same time, they say, people in a society have to believe that power is being used openly and for the benefit of everyone, rather than secretly and for the benefit of the few. While in practice power is fluid—so that at one moment a person may be in control and at another be controlled—ultimately there has to be a balance of power.

We cannot really ever escape power. Power is a fact of life. It is the energy that keeps the cogs of society turning; it is the give-and-take that governs all our relationships—at home, at work, and in political life.

Power need not be oppressive, however. We need to understand the forms that it can take and, where appropriate, question whether it is fair and just or not. We also need to make sure that in the long run we have the moral energy to make our own decisions and to shape our lives.

SEE ALSO: ABUSE, CLASS, CONFORMITY, CORRUPTION, DEMOCRACY, DISCRIMINATION, EQUALITY, MEDIA, OPPRESSION, POLITICAL CONDUCT, POVERTY, THREATS, VIOLENCE.

CRITICS OF POWER

One of the greatest critics of power in the 20th century was Michel Foucault (1926–1984). In books such as *Madness and Civilization* (1961) and *Discipline and Punish* (1975) Foucault argued that society uses power as a way of excluding some people and making the rest conform.

In the United States the thinker Noam Chomsky (b. 1928) argued that in modern democracies people are, in fact, powerless and that real power lies with a small, rich minority, or elite, that controls both the media and international business.

Praise

When we praise something or someone, we are saying that we approve of or admire that thing or person.

Praise and Moral Development

When someone does something that is morally good, she deserves praise. However, an act is only praiseworthy when the person who carries it out chooses to act in this way. If we are forced to tell the truth, for example, we do not deserve praise. Similarly, we are not blameworthy when we do something wrong because we are not free to do otherwise.

When a person praises another person, he may want to express approval for her action or to recognize and support her when she performs the morally right action.

From this we can see that praise may have a valuable role to play in moral development. The praise of someone else may encourage us to repeat a morally good action, just as being blamed for something wrong may discourage us from doing it again.

Doing the Right Thing

Once we learn what is right and wrong, however, we cannot rely on praise as a motivation to continue doing the right thing. For example, if a person is kind to others only because of the praise she will receive and not because she believes that it is the right thing to do, then she will probably not be kind when she is unlikely to receive praise.

There comes a stage in moral development where we act morally out of reason or conscience or some other moral motivations. If our only motivation to do the right thing is the expectation of praise, we would behave morally only when we thought others would notice and praise our actions, not from our own sense of right and wrong.

Once we have reached moral maturity, another's praise may be important as a way of reassuring us of the rightness of our actions or behavior, but it is not our primary reason for acting morally.

We also need to be wary of praise because sometimes people use it insincerely as a way of "buttering us up." We call this insincere praise flattery. Flattery does not make our behavior right and can lead us to misinterpret the effects of our actions on others.

Singing the Praises

When we praise someone who is our equal or our superior, then praise can become a form of respect. This is why in many religions it is customary to praise God. When Jews or Christians praise the Lord for being just or merciful, for example, they are reflecting on the moral rightness of such actions. They praise God for actions that would be praiseworthy for human beings to imitate.

In Africa there is a long tradition of "praise songs" in which not only the gods but people, animals, and the whole natural world can be the object of praise. These praise songs show what a community or people value: the courage of a warrior, the generosity of a leader, or the fertility of the land. In Western societies, too, the objects of our praise can be revealing about what we value in our society and environment.

SEE ALSO: ACHIEVEMENT, CONSCIENCE, CRITICISM, FLATTERY, MORALITY, VALUES.

Prejudice

People with disabilities often experience prejudice, yet many of them are able to live full lives despite their impairments. This man is using a computer with the aid of a capuchin monkey.

When we are prejudiced against someone, we make a judgment about her without basing that judgment on knowledge or facts. In other words, prejudice is an irrational opinion, thought, feeling, or attitude.

Judging before Thinking

Prejudice is a prejudgment. Say, for example, that Sharon is running for student government. Rex refuses to vote for Sharon because she lives in a "bad" neighborhood. He has not actually listened to what she has to say; he has simply dismissed her as a candidate because of where she lives. He is prejudiced.

Another word for prejudice is "bias." Prejudice, or bias, is not always negative. We can be biased in favor of something or someone. When a person is biased toward one person or thing, he is usually biased against its opposite. Some people place a high value on wealth, for instance, and are likely to judge someone by the amount of money she has. They are likely to be prejudiced against the poor and to think well of those who are wealthy, regardless of character or behavior.

Prejudice is a product of ignorance. It blocks growth and keeps people locked in closed ways of thinking. It often leads to

51

discrimination. Discrimination occurs when people are denied basic human rights because of such things as their race, gender, sexuality, religion, or nationality.

African and Asian people living in white societies often experience prejudice and are discriminated against in employment, housing, education, and certain club memberships. In some countries people are prejudiced against Jewish, Christian, or Muslim people. In practically all societies people with disabilities experience prejudice from others, particularly when applying for jobs.

Why Are People Prejudiced?

Children first learn their attitudes and beliefs from their families. Later they are influenced by their friends, schools, and television, newspapers, and magazines. If a person's family is prejudiced, that person is likely to be prejudiced too, at least at first. Later she may start to think for herself and question her beliefs and attitudes.

But some people never think about the beliefs they have picked up from their friends and family. Sometimes this is because they are never exposed to different ways of thinking. They continue to be prejudiced against others without questioning their own judgment, never wondering whether they are right to think this way.

Others use prejudice to cover up their own inadequacies and failings. They may be unhappy or dissatisfied with their lives. Instead of trying to work out how they might solve their own problems, they blame them on "outsiders," or scapegoats.

In history we have seen many examples of prejudiced people blaming others for their problems. In Nazi Germany (1933–1945), for instance, the Nazis blamed the Jewish people for many of Germany's problems.

Today people in many Western countries are prejudiced against foreigners who come to work in their country. They blame them for unemployment and poor living standards, saying "outsiders" are taking their jobs.

Can Knowledge Erase Prejudice?

Sometimes people change their views when they learn more about others. Some people who were racially prejudiced as children, for instance, may get to know and make friends with people from different racial groups when they get older. Their prejudices may decrease or even disappear.

But prejudice does not always respond to logic and reason. Many people cling to their prejudices even when confronted with knowledge that challenges their attitudes.

A white person, for instance, may believe that black people are athletic and great entertainers but not highly intelligent. When the white person is confronted with the reality of black heads of state, college presidents, and writers, she may maintain her prejudice by believing these are exceptions to the rule.

Similarly, a black person may believe all white people are oppressors. When he meets one who fights oppression, he holds on to his prejudice and maintains that this is the exception and not the rule.

Prejudice is understandable, given human nature and the many differences that exist in our world. However, it is harmful both to the person who is prejudiced and to the person who is being prejudged. We all need to learn to open our minds, to accept difference, and to learn the value of tolerance.

SEE ALSO: AFFIRMATIVE ACTION, ANTI-SEMITISM, ATTITUDE, BELIEF, DISCRIMINATION, HUMAN NATURE, JUDGMENT, LAW, OPPRESSION, RACISM, SEXISM, SNOBBERY, TOLERANCE.

Pride

We are proud when we have self-esteem or self-respect. Because such feelings can be justified or unjustified, pride can have either positive or negative meanings.

"Pride Comes before a Fall"

Sometimes proud persons are those who think of themselves as being better than or superior to other people or who have an exaggerated sense of their own abilities. Unrealistic self-esteem can sometimes get us into trouble. As a common saying puts it, "Pride comes before a fall."

The ancient Greeks illustrated this idea quite literally in the story of Icarus. Icarus's father, Daedalus, made him a pair of wings out of feathers held together with wax so that he could escape from prison. Icarus managed to escape but became so proud of his newfound ability that he flew too close to the sun. The wax on his wings melted, and Icarus fell into the sea and drowned.

The Greeks called extreme pride *hubris.* They believed that going beyond the limits set by nature or the gods was destructive. Overambitious politicians, they thought, often brought about their own downfall because they lacked proper respect for their citizens' freedom. The ideal, Greek thinkers said, was to be moderate in all things.

Most religions believe pride to be sinful because proud people lack proper respect for God. According to Catholic belief, pride is one of the seven deadly sins, for it means persons love themselves more than they love God. In the Bible pride is contrasted with the virtue of humility—the lack of arrogance or self-importance.

Taking Pride

Today, however, we often give pride a positive meaning. This kind of pride is justified self-esteem. In this sense Sadie would be right to be proud when after studying hard, she gets good grades. We are rightly proud, too, when we have confidence in our abilities and stand up for what we believe.

We can also be proud of our identity, sometimes in the face of long-standing prejudice. When someone is proud to be a Native American, for example, it means he values his culture. Someone can be proud of her sexuality, too. Many homosexual people take part in annual Gay Pride marches, at which they celebrate their pride in their identity.

SEE ALSO: ACHIEVEMENT, CONCEIT, HUMILITY, IDENTITY, MODESTY, SELF-ESTEEM, VANITY.

We are right to be proud when we have achieved something. These two students have just graduated and are showing their diplomas.

Privacy

"'If everybody minded their own business,' the Duchess said in a hoarse growl, 'the world would go round a deal faster than it does.'"

ALICE'S ADVENTURES IN WONDERLAND

All of us have a right to privacy—that is, the right to keep certain possessions, such as land and property, for our own use. We also have the right to keep certain private details to ourselves.

Our Private Lives

Although not all of us may own land, we are all owners of the personal details of our lives. Our private details include such things

As we grow older, our need for privacy increases. Sharing living space with others requires us to respect their need for privacy.

as who our parents are, who our friends are, our likes and dislikes, whom we voted for in the school elections, and so on. We may choose to keep these things to ourselves, or we may choose to reveal them to others.

Some people say that each of us needs to keep certain matters private to keep our sense of individuality. How would we feel if everybody knew everything about us?

Every person in the United States has a legal right to privacy. This means that other people do not have the right to make our intimate details public. Similarly, we do not have the right to ask our friends, neighbors, or teachers about details of their private lives.

The Right to Be Left Alone

In 1890 Supreme Court Justice Louis Brandeis said that privacy was "the right to be left alone." This right is suggested in the U.S. Constitution. The First and Fifth Amendments, for example, have to do with an individual's independence, his freedom to govern himself (autonomy), his right not to testify against himself in court—all matters that are directly related to privacy.

The Fourth Amendment protects the individual against unlawful searches and the unlawful taking of property. Privacy is freedom from unauthorized intrusion in our lives.

Extending the Right to Privacy

During our lives a lot of information about us accumulates in records kept by institutions such as hospitals, doctors' offices, schools, banks, and government agencies. Most of the time we do not know what these records say about us. They may contain information that is not true or that the institutions concerned do not need to know.

In the 1960s and 1970s many people in the United States became concerned that their records contained false information or that information about them would find its way to the wrong people. They put pressure on the U.S. government to prevent this, and in 1974 a new law of privacy was passed.

The U.S. Privacy Act of 1974 gave all American citizens the right to look at records kept by government agencies and institutions. The law stated that institutions and agencies could not give out information unless a court ordered them to do so, or certain other circumstances made it necessary.

But exactly how safe is our privacy? Technology has made it possible for more and more information about us to be collected and stored in computers and on microfilm. At the same time, though, technology has also made it easier for people to get information about us by electronic eavesdropping such as bugging phones and "hacking" into others' computers. It is difficult to control such invasions of our privacy.

Guarding Our Right to Privacy

Privacy, like our other rights and freedoms, is something we should value and fight to keep. It is everybody's responsibility to make sure that our right to privacy, and the right of others, is protected. We need to insure no one takes this right away from us.

Many people who are in the public eye—politicians, movie stars, supermodels, and pop musicians, for example—are constantly at risk of having their privacy invaded by the media. Editors, journalists, and photographers looking for stories about famous people often justify their actions by saying that the private lives of these people are in the public interest or that famous people have given up their right to privacy.

They may also say that it is the public who wants to read and view the stories they print and broadcast. If it did not, say the media people, they would not produce them.

Do these arguments on the part of the media justify invading people's privacy, particularly when it often causes the people concerned embarrassment and suffering? Does the public have a right to know? Or do individuals have a greater right to privacy?

SEE ALSO: BLACKMAIL, FREEDOM, GOSSIP, INDEPENDENCE, MEDIA, POLITICAL CONDUCT, REPUTATION, RIGHTS, SECRECY, SPYING.

Promises

When we commit ourselves to do something in either speech or writing, we are making a promise.

Making Promises

The most obvious way to make a promise is to say, "I promise." But we can also make a promise without using the word "promise," as when we say, "I'll do it. You can count on me." When we make a promise using words in this way, we are making an open, or explicit, promise.

We can also make implicit promises. A promise is implicit when we do not say it, but it is understood from the situation. For instance, when a teacher grades a class's papers, she has made an implicit promise to grade those papers fairly, simply by virtue of being the teacher of that class. And when students take a test, they also make an implicit promise not to cheat on their tests.

Similarly, when we are in a situation in which we are called on to give information, there is an implicit promise to tell the truth. If, for instance, someone asks us, "What time is it?" and we give a time that we know to be wrong, then we are breaking this implicit promise.

The ancient Greek philosopher Socrates (c. 469–399 B.C.) argued that everyone who lives in a country and continues to enjoy the protection of its laws has made an implicit promise to obey the laws of that country.

Swearing Oaths

Usually we make promises in a normal, everyday setting, not in a legal sense. However, in special circumstances persons may be called on to make a legally binding promise or oath. In these settings a person takes on a legal obligation (duty) as well as a moral obligation to do something.

For example, when people swear to tell the truth in a court of law, they promise under oath to tell the truth. Not telling the truth in a court of law after taking an oath is called perjury and is a serious crime.

Similarly, when a public official takes the oath of office, she swears to act in accordance with the responsibilities of that office. In doing so, she is promising in both an official and a legal way to perform the duties of her office. She takes on a moral and legal obligation to do what she has promised.

Breaking Promises

When we make a promise in an everyday setting, we have a moral duty to do what we have promised. Even if we have no legal duty, we certainly have a moral one.

We usually think of people who keep their promises as being dependable and trustworthy. On the other hand, we are not likely to trust people who habitually break their promises.

Some people argue that breaking promises devalues our language. If everybody, or even just a lot of people, broke their promises, no one would believe anybody who made a promise any more. Making promises would have no meaning.

However, there may be times when we ought not to keep a promise. Say, for instance, Doris makes a promise to help a friend with his work assignment at a certain time. On the way to his house, however, she

Treaties between nations are a kind of promise. Here U.S. President Ronald Reagan (right) and Soviet President Mikhail Gorbachev sign the 1987 Intermediate-range Nuclear Forces (INF) Agreement, by which the superpowers promised to reduce their nuclear weapons.

comes across a man who has hurt himself. In this instance her moral duty to stop and give aid to the man is more important—has a higher priority—than her promise to her friend, even though it means breaking her promise and letting the friend down.

If, however, Doris promises to help her friend and then simply decides to stay home and watch TV, she is not acting morally by breaking her promise.

Sacred Promises

Some promises have a sacred meaning. In many religions the exchange of marriage vows in a holy place, such as a church, mosque, or synagogue, is a promise made before God to love and be faithful to our spouse-to-be. If a person takes her marriage vows seriously, she believes that breaking those vows—by having other sexual partners, for example—will be a sin against God.

Jews believe that the whole relationship between God and human beings is based on a mutual promise, or covenant. In the Bible the Jewish god, Yahweh, undertakes to protect the Jews, and they undertake to obey him by keeping the Ten Commandments.

SEE ALSO: CONSCIENCE, DECEPTION, DUTY, LOYALTY, LYING, SPEECH, TRUST, TRUTH.

57

Protest

When we express our disagreement with or objection to a state of affairs, we are said to be protesting.

Forms of Protest

In daily life we often protest if we are told to do something we do not want to do. A teenager may protest to his parents about having to be at home at a certain time, for instance. We also use the word "protest" to describe people's objection to government policy, such as going on street marches.

Political protests raise many moral issues. Some people argue that in democratic societies ordinary people can cast votes in an election to get rid of a government they dislike and register their protest in this way. Since this is the case, they say, there is no need for other kinds of political protest.

Others point out that in practice, the system does not always work like this. They argue that political parties rarely offer real solutions to social problems, such as poverty and violence, and that even when parties come to power, they often go back on their promises. For this reason, they say, people need public protests to show the government that their demands cannot be ignored.

Most democratic governments uphold, at least in theory, their citizens' right to stage public protests on political issues. However, in practice governments often try to limit this kind of activity by passing special laws and by strict policing of such events.

Some people argue that it is the government's duty to prevent riots and public disorder of any kind. There is always the danger, they say, of some protesters becoming

These people are protesting against U.S. involvement in the Gulf War in 1991.

violent. Things can get out of hand, a riot starts, and innocent passers-by can be injured or even killed, they say.

Others are more suspicious of a government's motives. They argue that governments dislike public opposition and use the law and the police to stop any form of mass protest.

Nonviolent Protest

There are many kinds of public protest, but generally they can all be divided into violent and nonviolent methods. In the United States in the 1950s and 1960s civil-rights leader Martin Luther King Jr. (1929–1968) argued that nonviolent public protests were the best way for people to demand justice. He was inspired by Indian nationalist leader Mahatma Gandhi (1869–1948), who taught that it is our spiritual duty to protest against injustice in a nonviolent way.

King believed that a series of nonviolent public protests would help African Americans free themselves from racism and injustice without harming other human beings in the process. Today many people still believe in King's ideal of peaceful, or pacifist, public protest as a way of bringing about change without violence.

Other civil-rights leaders, such as Malcolm X (1925–1965), took a different view. He believed that African Americans had a moral duty to defend themselves against injustice and racism and that to do so they might have to use violence.

There are many different kinds of nonviolent protest that people can use to draw attention to important issues. These methods include public rallies, street marches, boycotts (refusing to buy goods from companies that discriminate against certain workers, for instance), strikes, sit-ins (in which protesters occupy an area prohibited to them), and walk-outs (in which large numbers of people walk out of a meeting, class, or office together in protest at what is being done there).

New Forms of Protest

As the issues affecting people change, new forms of protest have arisen to deal with them. For example, AIDS activists who are angry with the government for limiting funding for research have staged "die-ins" in public places. Hundreds of people lie down as if they were dead, stopping traffic.

Environmental activists chain themselves to trees in ancient forests to stop developers from cutting the trees down. And animal activists throw paint at people who wear fur to make them think about the suffering they cause to animals.

SEE ALSO: AIDS/HIV, DISCRIMINATION, OPPRESSION, PACIFISM, RACISM, REVOLUTION, RIGHTS, RIOT, TERRORISM, VIOLENCE.

VIOLENT PROTEST

Some forms of public protest encourage or use violence. The most extreme forms of violent protest are terrorist acts, such as hijacking aircraft or bombing public buildings with the intention of killing or injuring innocent people.

All terrorist activity involves serious criminal acts that harm other people. This kind of protest is quite different from peaceful protest and civil disobedience, and most people condemn it as morally wrong.

Other violent methods include making racist speeches at public meetings. Usually the speakers' intention is to whip up anger and hatred among the listeners, which often leads to violence.

Punishment

When someone in authority, such as a parent, teacher, or judge, imposes a penalty on someone for having done something wrong, we call this a punishment.

Types of Punishment

The form that a punishment can take varies greatly but usually matches the seriousness of the wrongdoing. When children do something wrong at home, parents often punish them by taking away privileges. They may, for example, ban them from watching television or from going out with friends.

At school teachers sometimes punish students by giving them extra assignments or by keeping them back after school. When the wrongdoing is particularly serious or violent, or when the student has done wrong more than once, he or she may even be expelled from school.

The most serious punishments are those imposed on persons who are found guilty of breaking a law—that is, of having committed a crime. In this instance the punishment usually takes the form of a fine, a prison sentence, or—in the case of very serious crimes such as homicide—the death penalty.

When the crime is a less serious or nonviolent one, the punishment can be a period of community service, such as helping take care of elderly people.

Corporal and Capital Punishment

Corporal punishment is punishment applied to the body, such as spanking or flogging. In traditional societies parents, teachers, and the law often used corporal punishment. In colonial times in North America, for example, criminals were sometimes publicly humiliated by being placed in stocks. And today some parents still use spanking as a way of punishing their children.

Some people argue that punishing children in this way is an effective way of teaching them right behavior. Many people believe that corporal punishment is a form of child abuse, however, and that it can be harmful to a child's well-being.

Capital punishment is punishment by execution and is sometimes called the death penalty. Capital punishment was once imposed for a great number of crimes. In 18th-century England, for example, there were several hundred crimes for which the death penalty could be imposed, ranging from petty theft to homicide.

Today, however, most countries use the death penalty only for very serious crimes, such as homicide and treason. Many countries have abolished the death penalty altogether. And in those countries that still impose the death penalty, there is a great deal of debate about whether capital punishment can ever be morally justified.

A Just and Proper Punishment

There are different views about what the aim of punishment should be. Some people say that a proper punishment should deter the wrongdoer and others from committing that offense in the future. According to this view, a proper punishment for stealing is one that deters potential thieves from stealing.

Others say that a proper punishment is one that seeks to change the behavior of the wrongdoer. In other words, this viewpoint

Today stocks are simply for our amusement, but in earlier times people used them to punish wrongdoers.

argues that a proper punishment should rehabilitate (correct) the wrongdoer so that he or she will do what is right in the future.

A third idea of punishment is that it should match the wrong: the more serious the wrong is, the greater the punishment should be. This very ancient principle is sometimes called by its Roman name, *lex talionis*.

Sometimes all of these ideas about punishment lead to the same outcome. If a child's parents catch her lying, they might punish her by sending her to her room. The next day she lies again, and this time her parents keep her in her room longer.

Each of the three ideas of punishment can explain why the parents should punish her this way. According to the first idea, a greater punishment is needed to stop her lying and perhaps to deter her younger brother from lying. According to the second idea, a greater punishment is needed to make her realize she is doing wrong. And according to the third, lying a second time is a more serious wrong than lying the first time.

Wrongful Punishment

People generally agree that cruelty and torture are unjustifiable forms of punishment, even if a person has done a very cruel wrong. The U.S. Constitution forbids "cruel and unusual punishment." Some people use this ban as an argument against capital punishment. Execution can cause psychological and physical pain before death, they say.

Punishment is not the same as revenge. A proper punishment is always carried out in the interests of justice and for the good of society as a whole. Revenge, on the other hand, is very often undertaken by someone directly affected by the wrongdoing (a relative of the victim, for example) who is taking the law into his own hands.

Many traditional communities, such as those in southern Italy, tolerate revenge, or vendetta. But one person taking revenge can lead to others taking revenge, setting in motion a deeply destructive cycle of violence.

SEE ALSO: BACKLASH, CAPITAL PUNISHMENT, CHILD ABUSE, CRIME, CRUELTY, DELINQUENCY, DETERRENTS, DISCIPLINE, JUDGMENT, JUSTICE, LAW, REVENGE, SPEECH, THREATS, TORTURE, VIOLENCE, WRONG.

Index

Volume numbers and page numbers for main entries are shown in **bold**.

Additional references to major subjects can be found in the SEE ALSOS at the ends of the entries.